CW01650404

CHARMING
SMALL HOTEL
GUIDES

Florida

CHARMING
SMALL HOTEL
GUIDES

Florida

Edited by Kathy Arnold & Paul Wade

DUNCAN PETERSEN

HUNTER
PUBLISHING INC

300 Raritan Center Parkway,
CN 94, Edison, N.J. 08818

Conceived, designed and produced by
Duncan Petersen Publishing Ltd

Editors	Kathy Arnold, Paul Wade
Principal inspector	Lans Christensen
Additional inspectors	Kate Dunning, Nanci Henchcliffe, Francie and Peter Hubbard, Kathryn Williams
Art director	Mel Petersen
Maps	Christopher Foley

This edition published in the UK and Commonwealth 1996 by
Duncan Petersen Publishing Ltd,
31 Ceylon Road, London W14 OYP.

Sales representation in the UK and Ireland by
World Leisure Marketing,
9 Downing Road, West Meadows Industrial Estate, Derby
DE21 6HA.

Distributed by
Grantham Book Services

ISBN 1 872576 58 3

A CIP catalogue record for this book is available
from the British Library

AND

Published in the USA 1996 by
Hunter Publishing Inc.,
300 Raritan Center Parkway, CN 94, Edison, N.J. 08818.
Tel (908) 225 1900 Fax (908) 417 0482

ISBN 1 556507 57 7

Typeset by Duncan Petersen Publishing Ltd
Originated by Reprocolor International S.R.I., Milan
Printed by G. Z. Printek, S.A.L., Bilbao

Contents

Introduction

Selection Process

Our selection of hotels, inns and bed-and-breakfasts has been made after thorough research, personal recommendations and expert assessment by a team of inspectors chosen by the editors.

No hotel, inn or bed-and-breakfast pays to be in this guide.

This is the eleventh book in the now well-established series of *Charming Small Hotel Guides*. In addition to France, Italy, Tuscany & Umbria, Spain, the British Isles, Germany, Austria, Switzerland and the New England region of the USA, we now move south to Florida.

Of all the *Charming Small Hotel Guides* written so far, Florida has the greatest diversity of places to stay that we have come across – from hotels and inns, to mansions and bed-and-breakfasts. Well-known for its gigantic hotels and endless concrete blocks of motels and condominiums, few realize, let alone believe, that charming small hotels exist. Yet we have found small luxury hotels hidden away on Miami's trendy South Beach, wood-shingled inns standing on deserted beaches, *Gone with the Wind*-style mansions surrounded by towering oaks and bed-and-breakfasts in the unexplored rolling hills and historic towns of central Florida. All represent American hospitality at its best.

Hotels, inns, and bed-and-breakfasts

Under the collective banner of Charming Small Hotels we list all types of accommodation. Many call themselves 'inns'. In the USA, that word conjures up an image of a white clapboard house on a village green, with fireplaces and plenty of antiques inside. This may be typical of New England, but inns have sprung up all over America.

In Florida, innkeepers, as the owners like to call themselves, have to battle with the cheap and cheerless chain motels that abound. They show off their antique furniture and take care over breakfasts; they offer up their knowledge of the area and bicycles to explore it; they are proud of a history that may be short by the standards of Europe or even New England, but is nonetheless significant in a state that celebrated its 150th birthday in 1996.

Our selections have around 25 bedrooms, some have fewer than ten. Even in Miami, our choices have no more than 60 rooms. Overall, they range from total luxury to honest simplicity.

We give our opinions on furnishings, atmosphere, value for money and the welcome. We are not fans of trouser presses or mini-bars stocked with expensive drinks; we prefer fresh flowers and a big smile. You should find plenty of both in this book.

Introduction

Entries
As in other books in the series, our warmest recommendations are given in full-page reports, complete with colour photographs. At the back of the book is a further selection of shorter entries. These have been inspected and are by no means 'second class' choices: they are *bone fide* charming small hotels, but, for one reason or another, do not justify a full page.

Bedrooms
Four-poster and canopy beds are commonplace in Florida's Victorian inns. Sizes range from double, to queen and king but some inns also offer twin bedded rooms. Many inns are converted old homes, so bedrooms come in all sizes; bathrooms are rarely spacious and can be tiny. Since Florida has long been a vacation destination, many seaside properties also offer small kitchens for the use of guests staying for several days

Meals
Breakfast may surprise first-time European visitors. Expect fresh fruits, muffins and breads as well as a 'special' of the day, perhaps pancakes or an egg dish. Breakfast may be served on a first-come, first-served basis or at a set time, at a communal or separate tables. If you have strong feelings about how you start the day, be sure to check exactly what is on offer.

Pets
Florida's inns rarely welcome pets. Always ask the innkeeper.

Electricity
Americans are on 110-120V, 60 cycles AC, using flat, two-pin plugs. Take the correct adaptor before leaving home.

Your host and hostess
Florida's innkeepers are enthusiastic and helpful. It is especially important to telephone in advance and to get precise directions.

Travel facts
The tourist information offices for each region are listed with the relevant maps a few pages further on.

Flights
Florida has several major international airports. These include Miami International; Orlando; Tampa, St Petersburg-Clearwater and Sarasota-Bradenton; Southwest Florida International at Fort Myers; Fort Lauderdale-Hollywood; Panama City, Pensacola and Tallahassee; Gainesville and Jacksonville; Daytona Beach and Melbourne; Key West.

Introduction

The award-winning airline Virgin Atlantic Airways operates three services from the UK to Florida: Gatwick to Orlando (daily), Gatwick to Miami (five days a week) and Manchester to Orlando (six days a week, except January 15 to March 15, when it is three days a week). Routes are served by Boeing 747 and Airbus A340 aircraft, which offer individual TV screens and a choice of channels to passangers in all classes. For flight information, contact Reservations (UK tel. 01293 747747).

Car rental

Value Rent-A-Car has 33 locations throughout Florida, and also rent in a further 17 locations in Georgia, Louisiana, Colorado, Arizona and Nevada. Value feature Mitsubishi models such as the Diamante, the Galant and the Eclipse as well as the Pontiac Sunbird and Cadillac Deville. Competitive rates for weekly rentals are available.

For reservations in the USA: tel. (800) GO VALUE
For reservations in the UK: tel. (0181) 876 9286

How to find an entry

We divide the state into three areas, starting with Southern, moving through Central to Northern Florida. Each area is broken down into smaller regions, each with its own map, marked with hotel locations and their page references.

The main, full-page entries are listed in alphabetical order by town. Finally, come the shorter entries again in regional order, again listed in alphabetical order by town.

There are three easy ways to find a hotel:

- Use the maps, pages 10 to 31. The numbers on the map refer to the page in the book where the hotel is listed.
- If you know the area you want to visit, browse through.
- Use the indexes at the back which list entries both by hotel name (p181-185) and by location (p 186-190).

How to read an entry

At the top of the page is the area of Florida; below that is the region; then follows the type of hotel, its town and, finally, the name of the hotel itself.

Fact boxes

Beneath each hotel description are the facts and figures which should help you to decide if the hotel is in your price range and has the facilities you require.

Tel and fax

The first number is the area code. The additional 800 area code is for toll-free calls made only in the USA and Canada.

Location

The setting of the hotel is described; car parking facilities follow.

Prices

The range of prices is from the cheapest single room in low season to the most expensive double in high season.

up to	$75	$
	$75 to $125	$$
	$125 to $175	$$$
	over $175	$$$$

A few hotels have rooms only within one price band. Do ask proprietors about reductions for longer stays. Some allow children to share a room; ask about the extra charge, if any. Always confirm prices when making a reservation and check how much local state taxes and gratuities add to the cost. When meals are served they are in relation to the cost of bedrooms. For a three-course meal for one person without wine, coffee, taxes or gratuities, expect to pay: up to $20 in a $ hotel; up to $25 in a $$ hotel; up to $35 in a $$$ hotel; $35 and over in a $$$$ hotel.

Rooms

Our lists of facilities in bedrooms do not cover ornaments such as flowers or extras such as toiletries.

Facilities

We list public rooms plus outdoor and sporting facilities. Public sports facilities and attractions near the hotel are under **Nearby**.

Smoking

Most hotels have restrictions; many are 'non smoking' inside, requesting guests to go outdoors to smoke.

Credit cards

We use the following abbreviations for credit cards:

AE American Express

DC Diners Club

MC Master Card

V Visa/Barclaycard/Bank Americard/Carte Bleue

A few of the smaller inns accept credit cards reluctantly, preferring cash or travellers' cheques.

Children

The age shown is our assessment of what is appropriate for that hotel. Always ask the innkeeper, however.

Closed

Florida is a holiday destination all year round. Very few hotels or inns close at all.

Gay Florida

Since Key West has a thriving gay community, we have included a special section listing those inns which are either exclusively or predominantly gay and lesbian. Find them on pages 155-156.

Florida

Florida is one of the most intriguing states of the USA. The 'Sunshine State', the nickname advertised on every car licence plate, has long been the land of beach vacations. Since 1971, however, Walt Disney World has put Florida on the international holiday map. Moreover, even those who have no desire to lie on a beach or cavort with Mickey Mouse have followed the NASA space programme whenever a rocket blasted off from Cape Canaveral. Yet Florida has far more history and culture than most visitors ever realize, a wider variety of landscapes than they ever bother to explore and a delicate eco-system in the Everglades that has world-wide importance.

While most of the USA looks to New England for the nation's historical roots, the Pilgrim Fathers were latecomers compared with Spanish explorer Juan Ponce de Leon. In 1513, more than a century before the landing at Plymouth, he named the land Pascua Florida, because he first sighted the coast at Easter. In 1565, another Spaniard, Pedro Menendez de Aviles, landed in northern Florida and founded the community of St Augustine. That town now trades on the title of 'longest established settlement in the New World'. After centuries of conflict, mainly with the British, Florida became part of the United States in 1821, and gained its statehood in 1845.

The next significant date is 1886 when railway tycoon Henry Flagler began building a railway line that would run the length of the entire East Coast. Later, in the 1920s, as northerners grew more affluent, so the land boom exploded, with plots sold both for retirement and holiday homes to Americans eager to escape bitter winters. During the Second World War, thousands more Americans were introduced to the year-round pleasures of Florida during military training. After the war, modern inventions furthered the prosperity. A system of freezing orange juice was perfected, while America's passion for beef helped boost the lot of the cattle ranchers of the Panhandle and Central Florida.

In recent years, Floridians have begun to put greater value on their history. 'Historic' is a relative term; in this state, buildings from the 1920s and 30s are often preserved, while town centres which escaped redevelopment in the 1960s are now tourist attractions in their own right.

This desire for old-fashioned character extends to holiday accommodation. Slowly but surely since 1990, Floridians and those from out of state have been restoring and renovating not just grand mansions and Victorian homes, but beachside villas and even modern blocks. Now, these offer a delightful alternative to the familiar highway motels, huge hotels on beaches, and the more recent phenomenon of the condominium.

Northerners have often booked in for weeks, even months

during winter, so kitchenettes, or at least a small refrigerator, are a familiar sight not just in suites but in bedrooms as well. The percentage of retired folk in the state is high, so many places have one room that is handicap accessible, some are even specially adapted. As for price, the southern part of the state has two seasons, but in the north, prices tend to be the same year-round. All over Florida, we found hotels, inns and bed-and-breakfasts that are attractive, well-run places to stay and deserve to be better known.

Main Florida holidays

January

New Year's Day	
Third Monday	Martin Luther King Jr Day (long weekend)

February

Second weekend	Lincoln's Birthday (long weekend)
Third weekend	Robert E Lee's Birthday (long weekend) (Presidents' Week, linking the two weekends, is often a school holiday)

May

Last weekend	Memorial Day (long weekend)

July

4th	Independence Day

September

First Monday	Labor Day (long weekend)

October

Second Monday	Columbus Day (long weekend)

November

First Tuesday	Election Day
11th	Veterans Day
Fourth Thursday, Friday	Thanksgiving Day Holiday

December

25th	Christmas Day

Florida

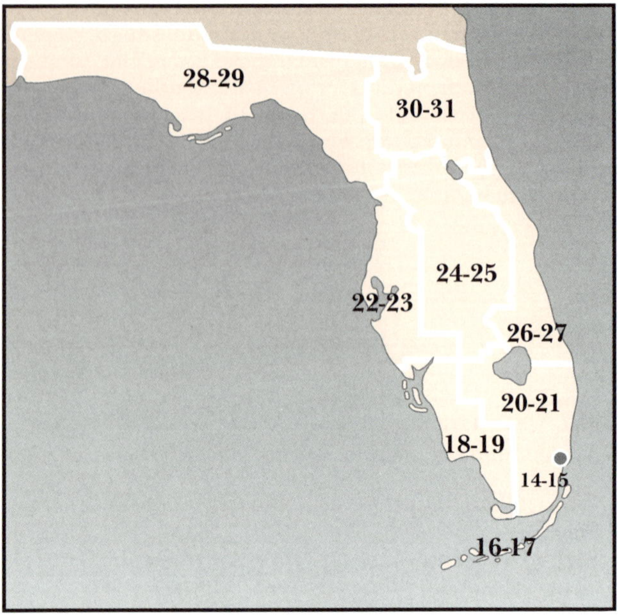

Key to maps of hotel locations and visitor information

Driving distances

Distances between main cities in miles

	Cocoa Beach	Daytona Beach	Fort Lauderdale	Fort Myers	Gainesville	Jacksonville	Key West	Kissimmee	Miami	Naples	Ocala	Orlando	Panama City	Pensacola	Sarasota	St. Augustine	St. Petersburg	Tallahassee	Tampa
Daytona Beach	65																		
Fort Lauderdale	165	229																	
Fort Myers	190	207	133																
Gainesville	155	98	312	230															
Jacksonville	153	89	317	285	69														
Key West	340	405	177	270	474	493													
Kissimmee	51	71	193	141	123	152	355												
Miami	186	251	22	212	331	338	155	212											
Naples	222	241	105	34	264	319	236	175	107										
Ocala	118	76	276	195	37	95	436	87	294	229									
Orlando	46	54	209	153	109	134	371	18	228	187	72								
Panama City	380	331	536	448	236	260	698	347	555	481	262	334							
Pensacola	473	425	630	541	330	354	792	441	649	575	356	428	103						
Sarasota	164	181	201	71	177	236	341	116	211	105	142	127	377	471					
St. Augustine	116	53	281	251	73	39	456	115	302	240	83	98	292	386	227				
St. Petersburg	142	159	234	110	143	208	379	95	245	141	113	105	342	435	39	197			
Tallahassee	288	234	444	356	144	163	606	255	463	389	170	242	97	191	285	195	250		
Tampa	122	139	234	123	128	188	387	74	245	156	93	85	331	425	53	177	20	239	
West Palm Beach	122	187	43	124	269	274	219	150	64	147	233	166	493	587	174	238	200	401	193

Greater Miami

Miami is a sprawling city. On the map, one community seems to run into another; on the ground, the differences are easy to see. Despite its popular image as a place of high-rise hotels, conference centres and cruise ships, we have found some outstanding small places to stay in three main areas: South Beach, Coral Gables and Coconut Grove.

Miami Beach is a long, narrow barrier island between the Atlantic Ocean and the spectacular Biscayne Bay. At the southern end is South Beach, often shortened to SoBe. For the past decade, this has been one of the world's most fashionable spots, thanks to the colourful art deco hotels. Built in the 1930s, these fell into disrepair after the Second World War. Renovated in the 1980s, their photogenic façades, coupled with the area's year-round sunshine, has attracted model agencies and photographers. Their presence draws young 'wannabes', who parade and roller blade along Ocean Drive, desperately hoping to be discovered.

This provides constant entertainment for the cafés on the terraces and in the former lobbies of the art deco hotels. It also means that bedrooms with views of the ocean are noisy unless they have sound-proofing. In general, less expensive hotels have the small bedrooms and tiny bathrooms of the 1930s, but in the last few years, luxury places have opened, which can rival New York or the south of France in style and services.

Coral Gables is totally different. Carefully designed in the 1920s, this is now a mature development in the elegant Spanish-Mediterranean style that has been copied right across America. Trees and gardens line the broad boulevards, restaurants are chic, the public swimming-pool looks like a Hollyood film set, but the Gables is also a thriving business area, only minutes from the airport and downtown.

Coconut Grove is often thought of as the Greenwich Village of the South, less opulent and affluent than Coral Gables and less frantic and funky than South Beach. There are café tables on the sidewalks, low-rise houses and a variety of shops but, more important, a real sense of a small community.

Miami's sun and sand are famous; its small hotels, restaurants and multi-cultural communities deserve to be better-known.

Greater Miami Convention and Visitors Bureau
701 Brickell Avenue
Suite 2700
Miami, FL 33131
Tel: (305) 539 3000; in USA only, (800) 283 2707
Fax : (305) 539 3113

Greater Miami

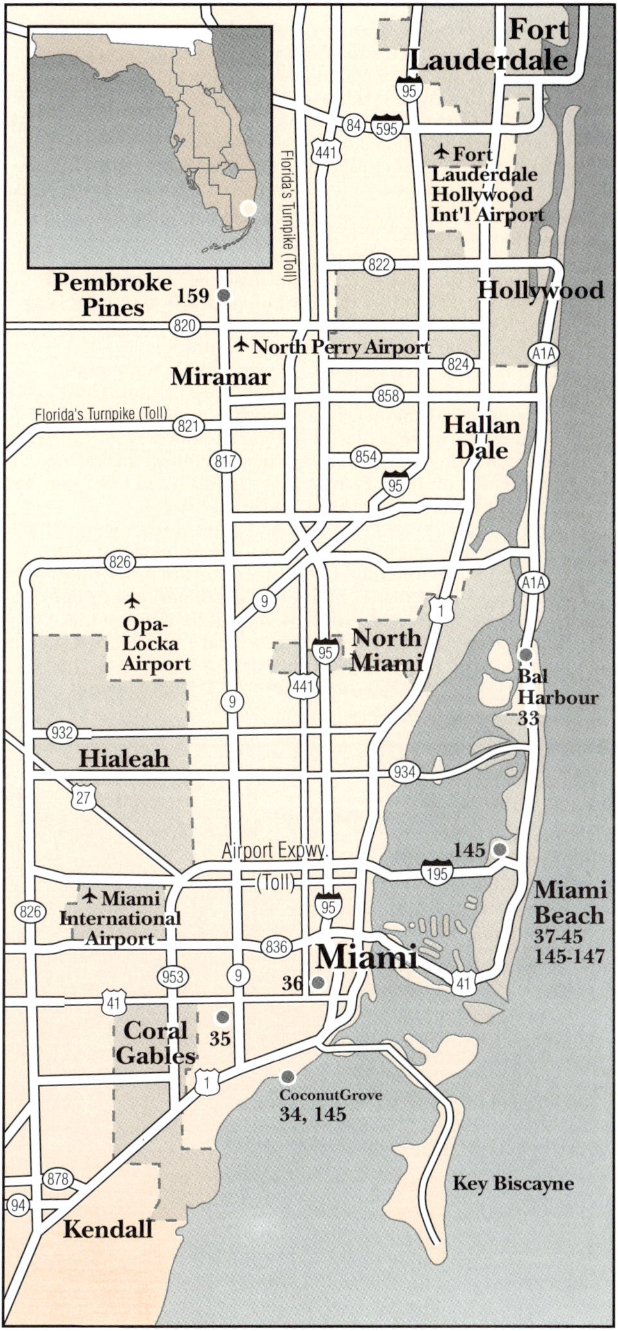

The Keys

The Florida Keys are a chain of coral rock islands, all linked by US 1, a narrow highway that runs from the mainland through the Upper Keys, the Middle Keys and Lower Keys to the world-famous small town of Key West. It takes about four hours to drive the 155 miles (250 km) from Miami to Key West, but heavy traffic at peak times can make this a laborious crawl. Although we include a few places to stay *en route*, including the exclusive Little Palm Island, the bulk of the small inns and bed-and-breakfasts are in Key West.

This is the southernmost point of the continental USA, just a few degrees north of the Tropic of Cancer, so the luxuriant gardens are full of exotic flowers. In the Old Town, shops, bars and restaurants line Duval, the main street, while century-old houses combine the gables of New England with the shady, airy porches of the American South. All the water sports are on offer and, of course, there are beaches for sunbathing.

The self-styled Conch Republic is proud of its Bohemian reputation. This dates back to the 1930s, when Ernest Hemingway spent time here with his artist and writer friends, but was reinforced by the growth of a strong gay community in the 1970s. In recent years, the atmosphere has become more mainstream; for example, the autumn Fantasy Fest carnival is enjoyed now by straight as much as by gay visitors and residents.

The range of bed-and-breakfasts and guest-houses is broad, so when booking a room, it is important to be frank about your expectations. Some welcome families, others are for couples only. Those with an 'all welcome' policy have both gay and straight guests, and may allow nude sunbathing. There are also places which are specifically gay. Therefore, we have, for the first time in the *Charming Small Hotel Guide* series, dedicated a small section (pages 155-156) to the best of the gay and lesbian bed-and-breakfasts and guest-houses.

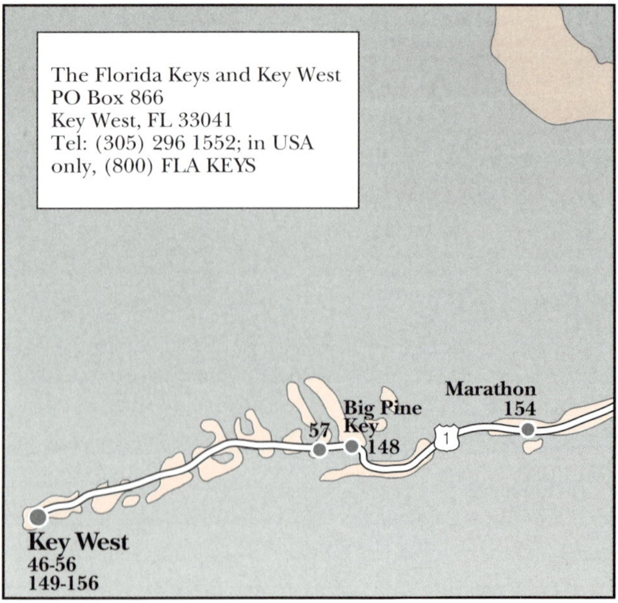

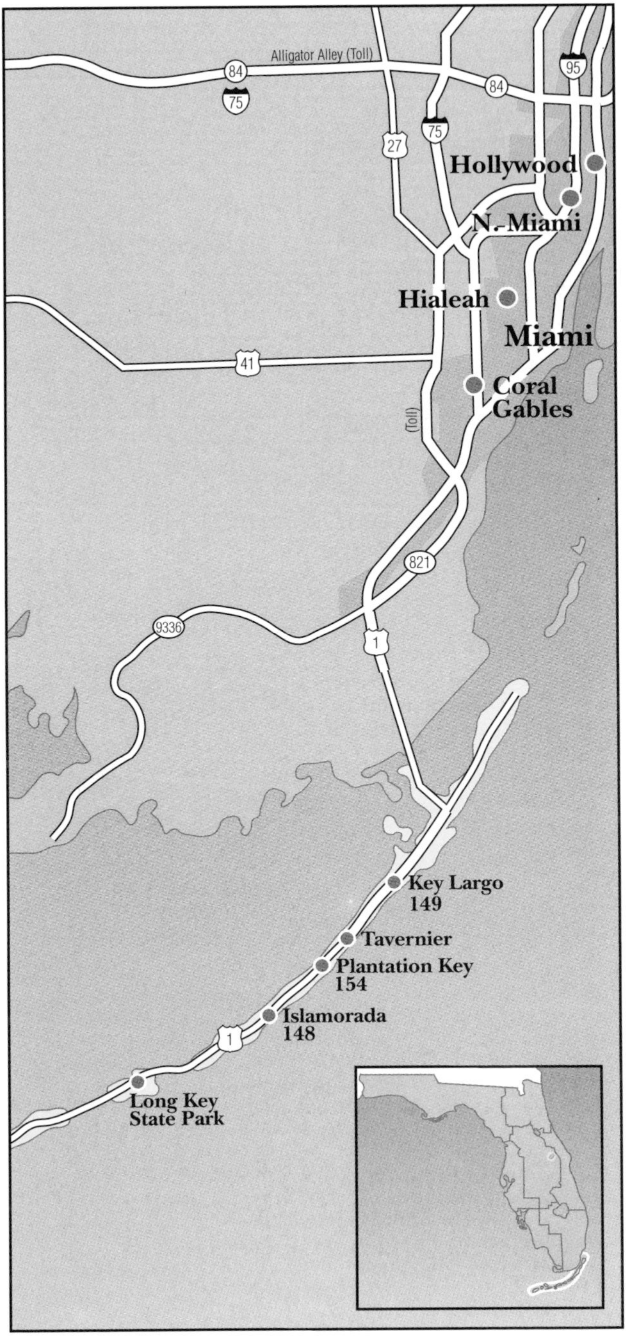
Alligator Alley (Toll)
84
75
84
95
27
75
Hollywood
N.-Miami
Hialeah
Miami
41
Coral Gables
(Toll)
821
9336
1
Key Largo 149
Tavernier
Plantation Key 154
Islamorada 148
1
Long Key State Park

Southwest

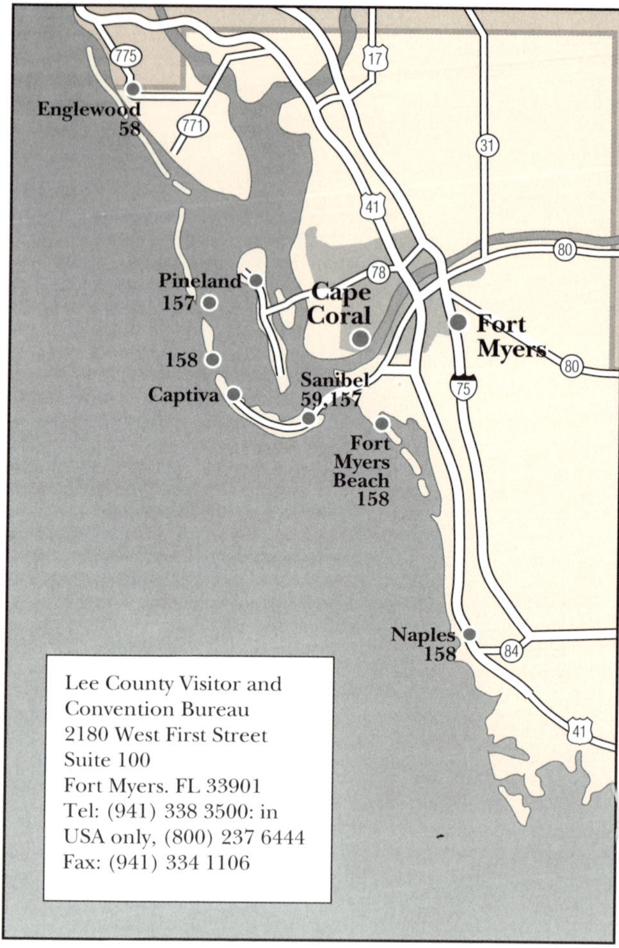

Southwest Florida is dominated by the Everglades in the south and some of the prettiest beaches in the state to the north. A series of barrier islands along the shore give this Gulf of Mexico coastline a special flavour, with bays and coves as well as shell-strewn beaches to explore. When it comes to finding charming small hotels, however, the area is thin on the ground. The dull motels that sprang up in the post-war period still provide inexpensive accommodation, alongside the more recent phenomenon of the condominium.

A delightful town such as Naples, for example, has just one bed-and-breakfast, and no small hotels at all. The islands off Fort Myers offer more choice. There are two recently-opened places on Sanibel, one of the most popular destinations in Florida, with its world-class beach. This island is linked by causeway to the mainland, but there are others, accessible only by boat, which offer a special experience.

Southwest

Marco Island & the Everglades Convention & Visitors Bureau
1102 North Collier Boulevard
Marco Island, FL 33929
Tel: (941) 394 7549; (800) 788 MARCO
Fax: (941) 394 3061

Naples Area Tourism Bureau
PO Box 10129
Naples, FL 33941
Tel: (941) 262 2712; (800) 605 7878
Fax: (941) 262 2113

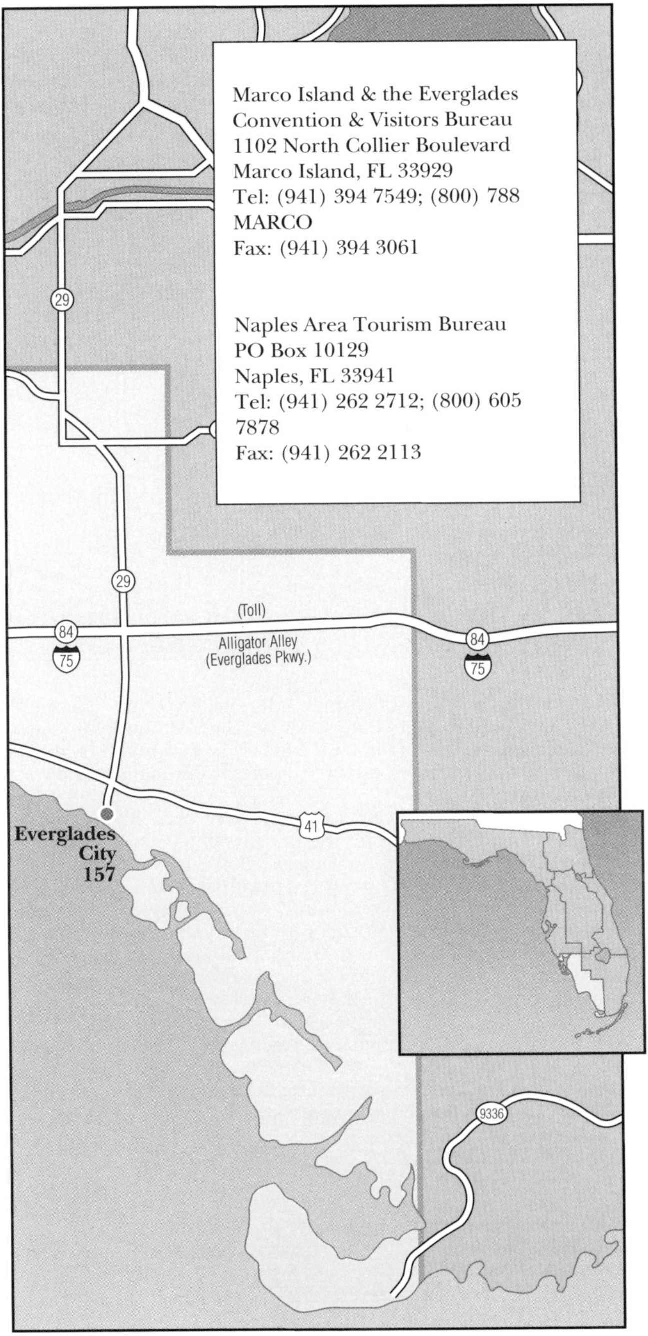

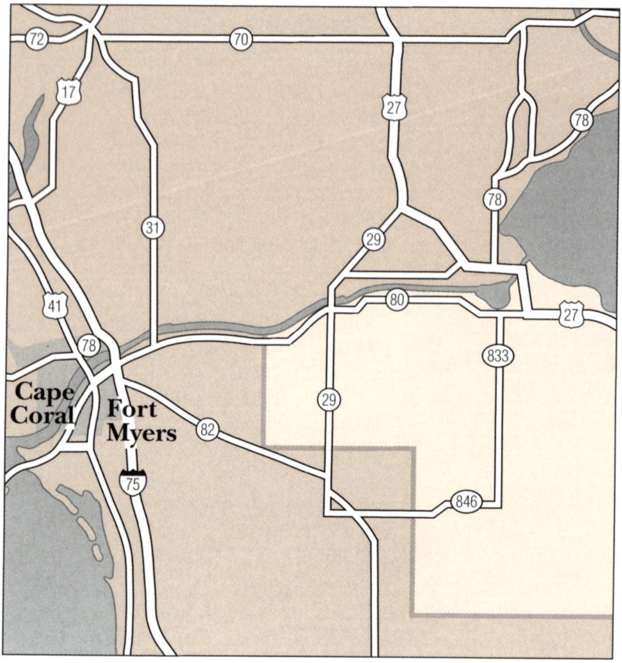

The southeast coastline of Florida is dominated by the Atlantic Ocean that pounds on to long sandy beaches. Although the state tourist board uses the 'southeast' label to include both Miami and the Keys, we have given these two important destinations their own sections.

Our Southeast area includes a variety of resorts. Most famous is Palm Beach, a playground for the wealthy for a century. Also well-known is Fort Lauderdale, a spring vacation destination for college students in the 1960s and popular ever since. To the north, Stuart is a low-key community, which prides itself on being 'the sailfish capital of the world', with fine, relatively empty beaches nearby on Hutchinson Island. Although Floridians often come here for a break, it is less known to other Americans, let alone to international visitors. Slowly but surely small inns are opening up in the shadow of the giant hotels, responding to a demand by discerning guests for a return to old-fashioned values.

Greater Fort Lauderdale Convention & Visitors Bureau
200 East Las Olas Boulevard Suite 1500
Fort Lauderdale, FL 33301
Tel: (954) 765 4466; in USA only, (800) 22 SUNNY
Fax: (954) 765 4467

Palm Beach County Convention & Visitors Bureau
1555 Palm Beach Lakes Boulevard Suite 204
West Palm Beach, FL 33401
Tel (407) 471 3995; in USA only, (800) 544 7256
Fax: (407) 471 3990

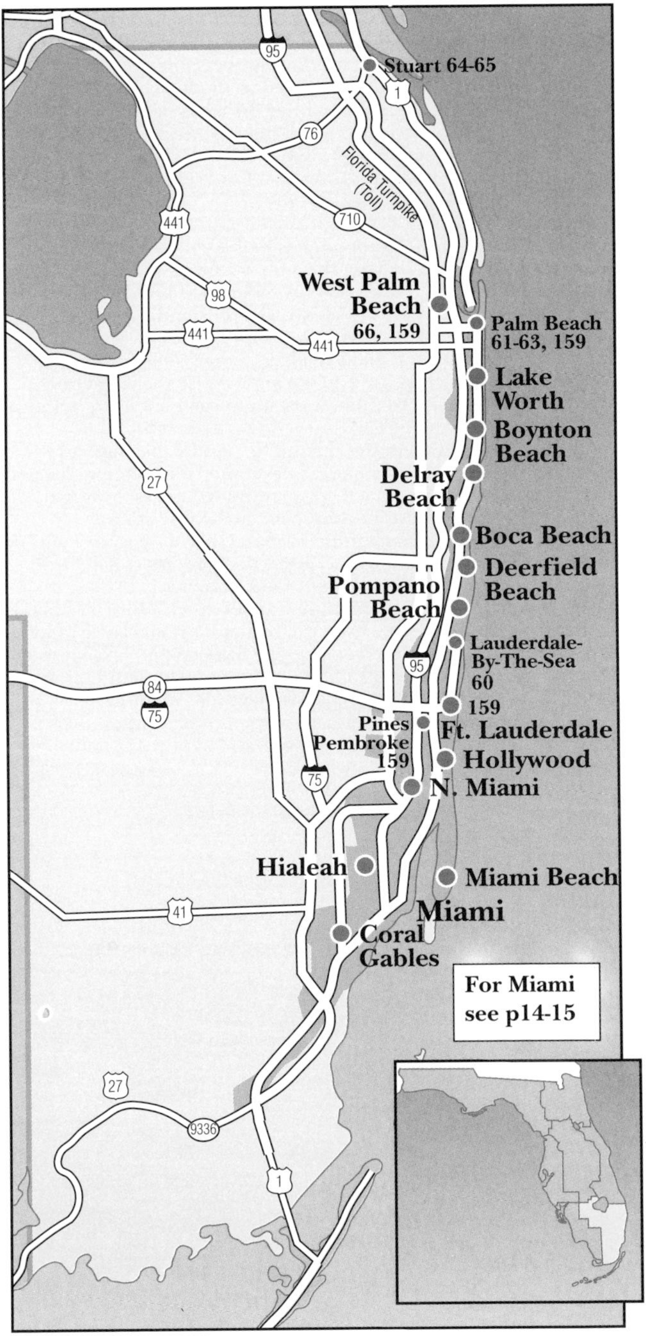
95
Stuart 64-65
1
76
Florida Turnpike (Toll)
441
710
98
West Palm Beach 66, 159
441
441
Palm Beach 61-63, 159
Lake Worth
Boynton Beach
27
Delray Beach
Boca Beach
Deerfield Beach
Pompano Beach
Lauderdale-By-The-Sea 60
95
84
75
159
Pines Pembroke 159
Ft. Lauderdale
Hollywood
75
N. Miami
Hialeah
Miami Beach
41
Miami
Coral Gables
For Miami see p14-15
27
9336
1

Central West

Beaches here are the sort seen on posters. Long and clean, with white sugar-soft sand, they border the string of islands that continues up the coast from the Southwest. Some are clumped together under an umbrella title, such as the Beaches of St Petersburg. Others, such as Siesta Key off Sarasota and Holmes Beach off Bradenton may be known only to aficionados. The amount of development varies dramatically, with large hotels giving way to residential areas, and fast food restaurants ending at the start of an historic district.

The main cities of St Petersburg, Tampa and Sarasota offer major league sports and shopping as well as culture. In St Petersburg, the Salvador Dali Museum is a must, while in Sarasota, circus-owner John Ringling used his millions to build a Venetian-style palace on the waters of the bay. His outstanding collection of Old Masters is here, as is a theatre, shipped piece by piece from Italy and rebuilt. Off the main roads are small, delightfully old-fashioned towns such as Tarpon Springs, whose thriving Greek community dates back to the start of the sponge industry in the early 1900s.

At the northern end of the region, the landscape changes. Offshore islands here are small, undeveloped and often dedicated to nature reserves. The crystal-clear spring-fed rivers flowing into the Gulf of Mexico provide a home for the extraordinary manatee, a lovable, though homely, mammal called a mermaid by homesick pirates. Inland, the countryside becomes rolling, with pine and oak trees, fruit farms and cattle ranches.

Although there are few traditional small hotels, there are plenty of charming places to stay. As in the rest of Florida, century-old houses have been renovated and opened as bed-and-breakfasts. There is also a movement to upgrade and redecorate buildings dating from the 1950s and 1960s. We have also included a number of attractive self-catering places, mostly right on the water. All have the character and ambience expected of any recommendation in the *Charming Small Hotel Guides*.

Bradenton Area Convention & Visitors Bureau
PO Box 1000
Bradenton, FL 34206
Tel: (941) 729 9177; in USA only, (800) 4 MANATEE
Fax: (941) 729 1820

St Petersburg/Clearwater Area Convention & Visitors Bureau
One Stadium Drive, Suite A
St Petersburg, FL 33705
Tel: (813) 582 7892; in USA only, (800) 345 6710
Fax: (813) 582 7949

Sarasota Convention & Visitors Bureau
655 North Tamiami Trail
Sarasota, FL 34236
Tel: (941) 957 1877; in USA only, (800) 522 9799
Fax: (941) 951 2956

Tampa/Hillsborough Convention & Visitors Association
111 Madison Street, Suite 1010
Tampa, FL 33602
Tel: (813) 223 2752; in USA only, (800) 44 TAMPA
Fax: (813) 229 6616

Central West

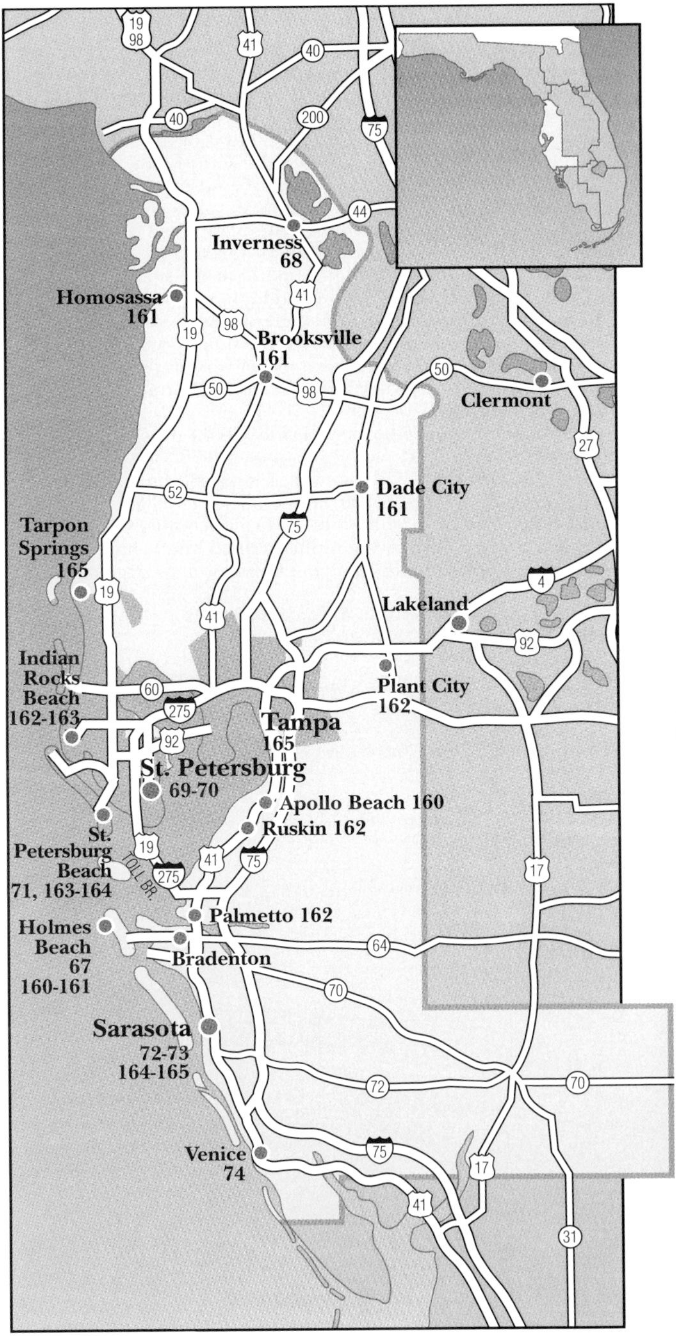

Central

Of all the regions, this must be the most deceptive. After all, the sprawling city of Orlando dominates, with its Walt Disney World attractions a magnet to every child on earth. Our inspectors, however, found small hotels and bed-and-breakfasts with considerable character even in the shadows of the 1,000-room hotels. What is more, they explored the countryside around Orlando and found not just a variety of landscape but attractive towns, botanic gardens and nature parks.

Just an hour or so away from Orlando are small historic communities such as Bartow, Eustis and Lakeland. Lake Wales boasts Iron Mountain, the highest point in the state at 298 ft (90 m) above sea level, while the second-highest point is lakeside Mount Dora. Suprisingly reminiscent of New England towns, it is known in the Southeastern USA for the quality of antiques on offer in its numerous shops. Even more suprising are the stallions at stud around Ocala, where winners of the Kentucky Derby are often born and bred.

Few first-time time visitors expect to see the 1,000 or more lakes north of Orlando. Some are for fishing, others for water-skiing, a few are for swimming and many are for just sitting and looking at.

Throughout this region, our inspectors were delighted by the small hotels and inns, with enthusiastic, welcoming owners and staff determined to show the multi-national hotel chains that American hospitality can come in small as well as large packages.

Central Florida Convention & Visitors Bureau
600 North Broadway, Suite 300
Bartow, FL 33830
Tel: (941) 534 4370; in USA only, (800) 828 7655
Fax: (941) 533 1247

Kissimmee-St Cloud Convention & Visitors Bureau
PO Box 422007
Kissimmee, FL 34742
Tel: (407) 847 5000; in USA only, (800) 327 9159
Fax: (407) 847 0878

Orlando/Orange County Convention & Visitors Bureau
8445 International Drive
Orlando, FL 32819
Tel: (407) 363 5892
Fax: (407) 363 5899

Central

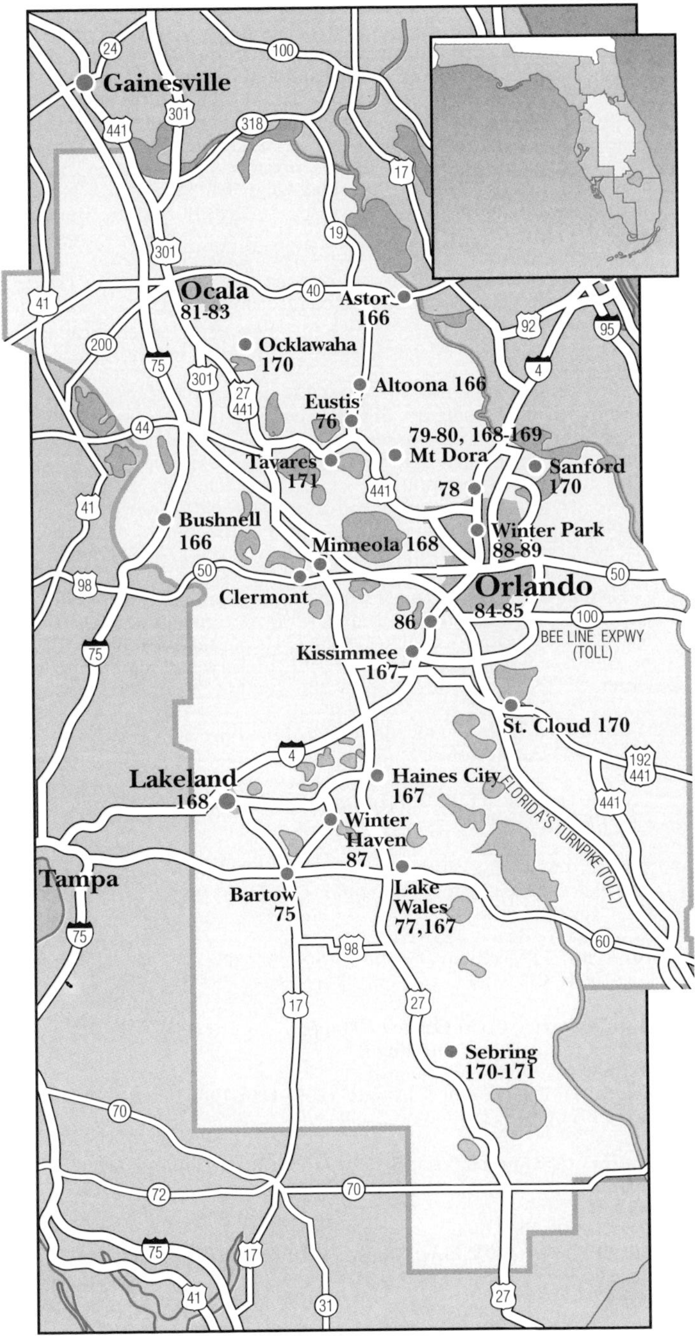
Gainesville
Ocala
81-83
Astor
166
Ocklawaha
170
Altoona 166
Eustis
76
79-80, 168-169
Mt Dora
Tavares
171
Sanford
170
78
Bushnell
166
Winter Park
88-89
Minneola 168
Clermont
Orlando
84-85
86
BEE LINE EXPWY
(TOLL)
Kissimmee
167
St. Cloud 170
Lakeland
168
Haines City
167
FLORIDA'S TURNPIKE (TOLL)
Winter
Haven
87
Tampa
Bartow
75
Lake
Wales
77,167
Sebring
170-171

Central East

This long, thin sliver of a region depends for its popularity on the Atlantic beaches and the barrier islands that line the shore. In the north, Daytona Beach rose to international fame thanks to the broad expanse of hard sand used by dare-devil drivers at the turn of the century for attempts on the world speed record. Today, the Speedway, a vast concrete bowl, pulls in huge crowds to watch cars and motorbikes contest well-known endurance races such as the Daytona 500 and Daytona 200 (mile) races. The beach, however, is the focus for thousands of university students during the March spring break.

At the mid-point of the region is Cape Canaveral, known around the world since 1958 for its space launches; Explorer 1, the USA's first earth satellite blasted off from here. Our inspector found an inn where you can watch the latest rockets blast off in to space from the comfort and convenience of your bedroom balcony.

Less well-known is the Intracoastal Waterway, the channel running parallel to the ocean where boats can circumnavigate the coast in safety. It runs between the barrier islands and the mainland before turning inland at Stuart, crossing Lake Okeechobee and reaching the Gulf of Mexico at Fort Myers. There are several places to stay with attractive views over this calmer expanse of water; some were once the homes of the men and women, such as bridge keepers, who worked to keep traffic flowing smoothly.

Fishing is as popular a recreation as sunbathing and swimming at the beaches along this shoreline, while away from the coast are less well-known towns such as DeLand, where some 300 old houses have been carefully and proudly preserved along the main street.

Daytona Beach Area Convention & Visitors Bureau
126 East Orange Avenue
Daytona Beach, FL 32114
Tel: (904) 255 0415; in USA only, (800) 854 1234
Fax: (904) 255 5478

East Central Tourism Bureau
(for New Smyrna Beach, Edgewater, Oak Hill)
115 Canal Street
New Smyrna Beach, FL 32168
Tel: (904) 428 2449; in USA only, (800) 541 9621
Fax: (904) 423 5729

Florida's Space Coast Office of Tourism
2725 St Johns Street, Building C
Melbourne, FL 32940
Tel: (407) 633 2110; in USA only, (800) USA 1969
Fax: (407) 633 2112

The Tourist Council, Vero Beach/Indian River County Chamber of Commerce
1216 21st Street
Vero Beach, FL 32960
Tel: (407) 567 3491; in USA only, (800) 338 2678 ext 802
Fax: (407) 778 3181

Central East

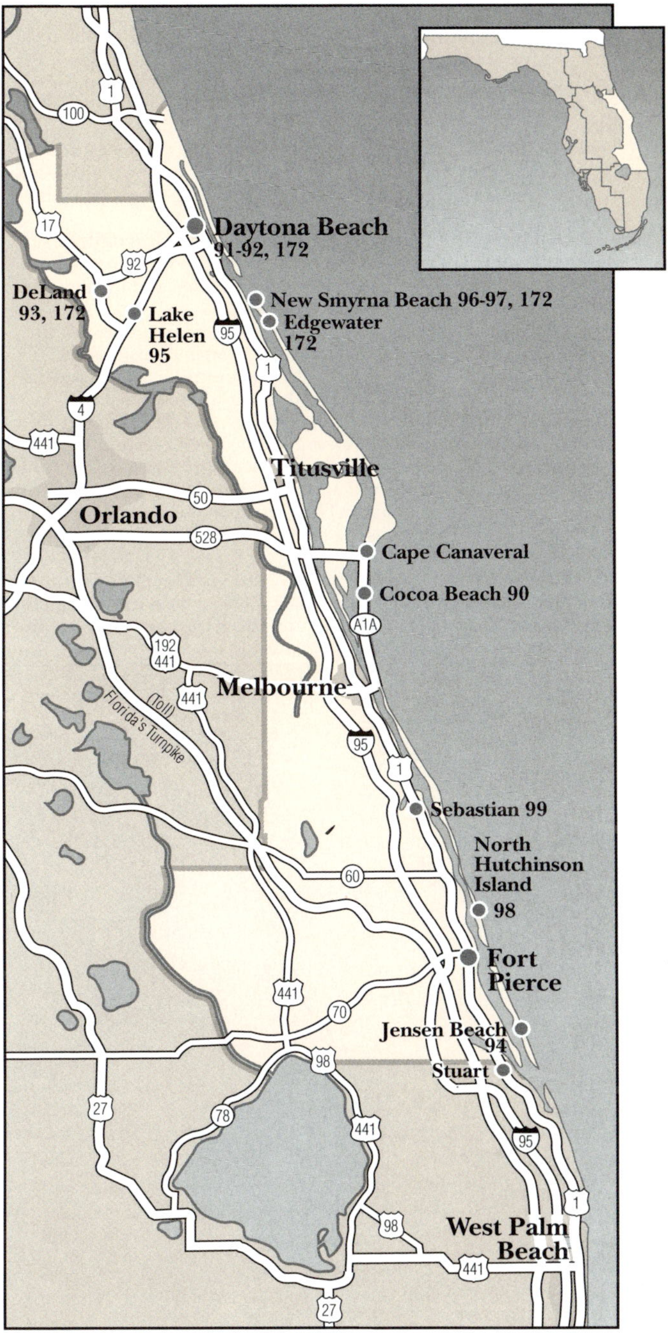

Northwest

This is a huge sprawling section of Florida, from Pensacola in the west, on the Alabama border, right across to the Suwannee River, enshrined in the popular song, *Way down upon the Suwannee River.* All along the Gulf Coast are superb beaches plus a couple of islands, St George Island and Cedar Key, which are noticeably less-developed than those further south. There are few small hotels among the motels, but the mock-Victorian town of Seaside is at the forefront of the battle to restore a little character to the coast.

The old towns of Pensacola and Apalachicola, by contrast, do have atmosphere, thanks to the preservation of old houses and warehouses, while Tallahassee has the affluence and bustle befitting a state capital.

North of the capital are the reminders of the plantations, the gigantic estates built before the Civil War, with mansions to match. Explorers who search for this southern charm, as well as antiques, often go to pleasant small towns such as Havana, Monticello and Thomasville. Thomasville is, in fact, a few minutes drive over the state line into Georgia. Because of its popularity, however, we have included several bed-and-breakfasts there. They are historic, comfortable and a useful addition for anyone touring the northern edge of Florida. They are also handy when college football games in Tallahassee or Jacksonville put a premium on accommodation.

Northern Florida is so wide that it extends into the next time zone. The line is around Apalachicola. The region to the west, up to the Alabama border, is on Central Time, one hour behind the rest of the state, which is on Eastern Time.

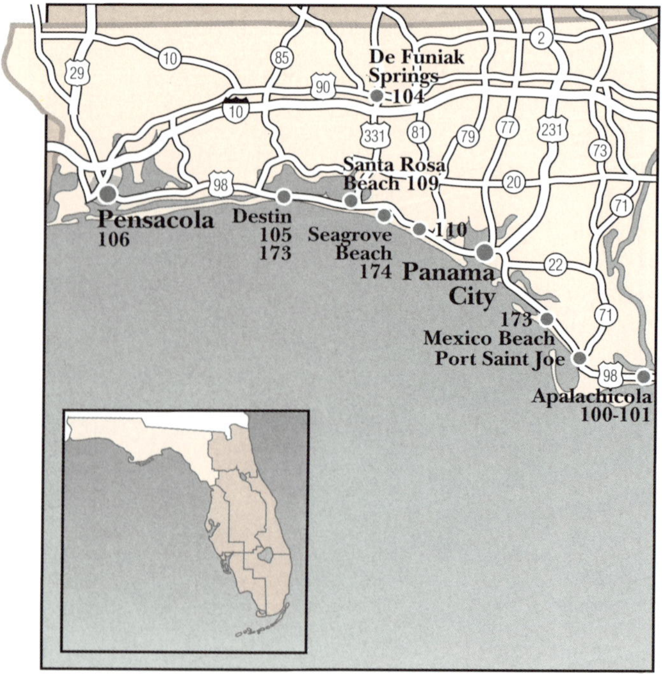

Northwest

Pensacola Convention & Visitors Information Center
1401 East Gregory Street
Pensacola. FL 32501
Tel: (904) 434 1234; in USA only, (800) 874 1234
Fax: (904) 432 8211

South Walton Tourist Development Council
PO Box 1248
Santa Rosa Beach, FL 32459
Tel: (904) 267 1216; in USA only, (800) 822 6877
Fax: (904) 267 3943

Tallahassee Area Convention & Visitors Bureau
200 West College Avenue
Tallahassee, FL 32301
Tel: (904) 413 9200; in USA only, (800) 628 2866
Fax: (904) 487 4621

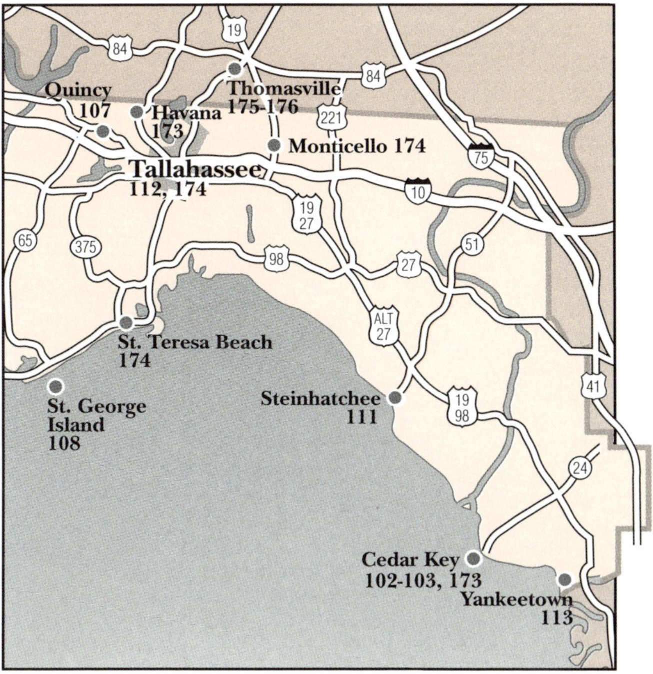

Northeast

The Spanish names of the towns proclaim that this is where Europeans settled more than 430 years ago. The most famous, St Augustine, trades on its history and has numerous bed-and-breakfasts in the Historic District. Unfortunately, the town's popularity has led to a rather casual attitude to innkeeping, and our inspector was disappointed to find a number of inns that desperately need a facelift. So, although he looked at many, he chose only a few.

Up in the northeast corner, Amelia Island and Fernandina

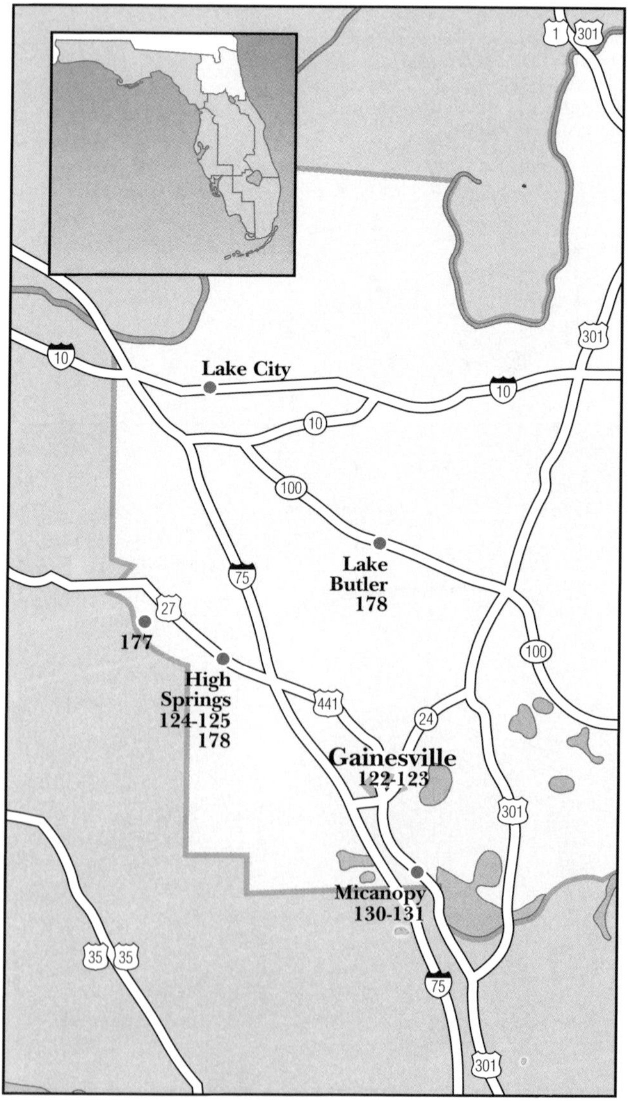

Beach attracts families as well as couples taking a break. Inland are lively cities such as Jacksonville, working hard to preserve its historic district on the St Johns River, and Gainesville, voted the 'best place to live' in the USA. High Springs and Micanopy are villages whose old-Florida style deserves to be better known.

Amelia Island Development Council
102 Centre Street
Fernandina Beach, FL 32035
Tel: (904) 277 0717; in USA only, (800) 226 3542
Fax: (904) 261 6997

Jacksonville & the Beaches Convention & Visitors Bureau
3 Independent Drive
Jacksonville, FL 32202
Tel: (904) 798 9148; in USA only, (800) 733 2668
Fax:: (904) 798 9103

St Augustine Chamber of Commerce
1 Riberia Street,
St Augustine, FL 32084
Tel: (904) 829 5681
Fax: (904) 829 6477

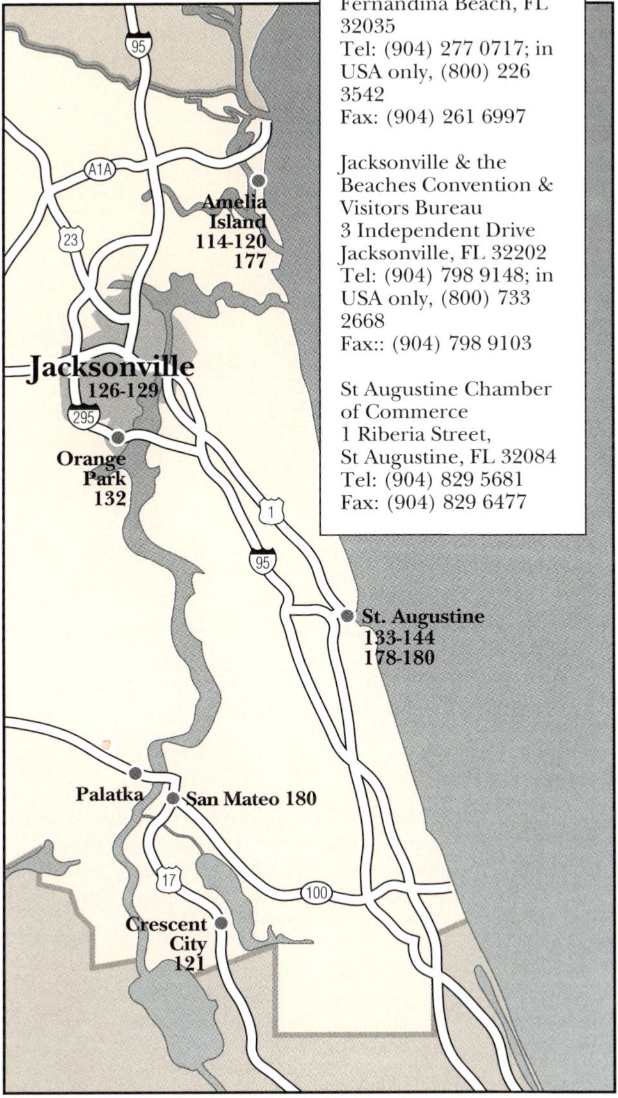

Reporting to the guides

Please write and tell us about your experiences of small hotels, bed-and-breakfasts and inns, whether good or bad, whether listed in this edition or not. As well as hotels in Florida, we are interested in charming small hotels in: Britain, Ireland, Italy, France, Spain, Portugal, Germany, Austria, Switzerland and other European countries, as well as New England and the west coast of the United States.

The address to write to is:
The Editors
Florida
Charming Small Hotel Guides
Duncan Petersen Publishing Ltd.
31 Ceylon Road
London W14 0YP
England

Checklist
Please use a separate sheet of paper for each report; include your name, address and telephone number on each report.

Your reports will be received with particular pleasure if they are typed, and if they are organized under the following headings:

Name of establishment
Town or village it is in, or nearest
Full address, including post code
Telephone number
Time and duration of visit
The building and setting
The public rooms
The bedrooms and bathrooms
Physical comfort (chairs, beds, heat, light, hot water)
Standards of maintenance and housekeeping
Atmosphere, welcome and service
Food
Value for money

We assume that in writing you have no objection to your views being published unpaid, either verbatim or in an edited version. Names of major outside contributors are acknowledged in the guide, at the editors' discretion.

Greater Miami

Waterside hotel, Bay Harbor Islands

Bay Harbor Inn

Miami Beach is a long barrier island with a variety of developments. At one end is trendy, noisy South Beach, in the middle are huge hotels, and at the northern tip is Bay Harbour Village, an upmarket area known for designer shopping. Within walking distance, but on one of the islands in Biscayne Bay, stands the inn. Built as an hotel in 1948, a green awning marks the entrance while inside, the rather plain Victorian-looking foyer has potted plants on a hardwood floor and an old pigeon-hole mailbox for brochures. This is Townside, whose Palm Restaurant is an offshoot of New York's 70-year old landmark.

Bedrooms are comfortable, with reproduction furniture and modern, practical bathrooms. Across the road, in the more contemporary Creekside building, the ambience is more Floridian. Rooms here have broad balconies with views of the Intracoastal Waterway, the swimming-pool and yacht *Celeste*, the barge-like vessel that makes an unusual breakfast-room.

Not everyone wants the self-conscious atmosphere typical of many South Beach hotels. For such holidaymakers and business travellers, this straightforward inn offers a sedate alternative.
Nearby shopping, water sports; Miami.

9660 East Bay Harbor Drive, Bay Harbor Islands, FL 33154
Tel and Fax (305) 868 4141
Location off Broad Causeway, on northern Biscayne Bay; ample car parking
Meals breakfast, lunch, dinner
Prices rooms $-$$$$ with breakfast
Rooms 24 double; 12 suites; all have bath or shower, air-conditioning, phone, TV
Facilities 2 restaurants, breakfast-room, 2 sitting-rooms, bar, lift/elevator; garden, heated outdoor swimming-pool
Smoking permitted
Credit cards AE, DC, MC, V
Children welcome
Disabled not suitable
Closed never
Languages English only
Manager Lee Machett

Greater Miami

Waterside hotel, Coconut Grove

Grove Isle Club and Resort

Once Miami's best-kept secret, Grove Isle's hotel blossomed into a small luxury resort late in 1994 with a line up of stars to match its stunning setting on Biscayne Bay. Roscoe Tanner oversees the tennis program while Mark Militello, one of America's leading chefs, supervises one of the restaurants.

A tiny island five minutes east of Coconut Grove, Grove Isle is approached via a bridge and a security checkpoint. The 12 tennis courts, swimming-pool, 85-slip marina and other sports facilities are used by residents of the three condominium blocks as well as guests at the resort. Well-known designer Lynn Wilson upgraded the hacienda-style bedrooms from comfortable to deluxe, retaining terracotta floor tiles but adding caramel-coloured mahogany furniture. In the all-white bathrooms, dramatic black marble surrounds the wash-basins. The decorative master plan continues in the public areas with striking original art, enormous flower arrangements and, in the indoor restaurants, panoramic views across manicured lawns to the water. With the services of a top city hotel plus executive conference facilities, the overall package aims at the top of the market, with prices to match.

Nearby Vizcaya, Coconut Grove, water sports.

4 Grove Isle Drive, Coconut Grove, Miami, FL 33133
Tel (305) 858 8300; (800) 88 GROVE
Fax (305) 854 6702
Location on private island; ample car parking
Meals breakfast, lunch, dinner, snacks
Prices rooms $$$$; charge for breakfast
Rooms 40 double; 9 suites; all have bath or shower, air-conditioning, phone, TV, VCR, hairdrier, safe
Facilities 2 dining-rooms; lift/elevator; outdoor café, garden, fitness area, heated swimming-pool, tennis courts
Smoking restricted
Credit cards AE, DC, MC, V
Children very welcome
Disabled 2 adapted rooms
Closed never **Languages** French, Italian, Spanish
Proprietor Bernard Lerner

Greater Miami

Town hotel, Coral Gables

Place St Michel

The city of Coral Gables is a perfect example of successful town planning. Back in the 1920s when it was started, the Mediterranean-looking houses were a new style in Florida; only their popularity has turned them into architectural clichés. Now, the exotic mahogany, balsa and kapok trees that were planted along the broad boulevards have matured into botanic garden specimens. Although the integrity of the residential development has been strictly maintained, the authoritarian city council has welcomed multi-national companies to the small business district.

Right in its heart is the Place St Michel, built in 1926. " It feels like a small hotel in Paris," declared a French businessman, who felt at home with the dark wood panelling, art deco lamps and antique elevator. Even Stuart's Bar, where regulars meet up for a glass of wine after work, is more Montparnasse than Miami. A fire in the kitchen in 1995 provided an excuse to refit the air-conditioning and upgrade the bathrooms. The comfortable but deliberately old-fashioned bedrooms, however, have changed little; they still have 1930s beds and wardrobes from France, and sewing machine tables under the TV sets.

Nearby beach, shopping, Venetian Pool, University of Miami.

162 Alcazar Avenue, Coral Gables, FL 33134
Tel (305) 444 1666; (800) 848 HOTEL
Fax (305) 529 0074
Location corner of Alcazar and Ponce de Leon Blvd; public car park across the street
Meals breakfast, lunch, dinner, snacks
Prices rooms $$$-$$$$ with breakfast
Rooms 24 double; 3 suites; all have bath or shower, air-conditioning, phone, TV
Facilities dining-room, bar, lift/elevator
Smoking restricted
Credit cards AE, MC, V
Children welcome
Disabled not suitable
Closed never
Languages English only
Manager Christian Horsley

Greater Miami

Historic bed-and-breakfast, Downtown Miami

Miami River Inn

Sallye Jude is an optimist and a believer in the best of human nature. "People thought I was mad to open a bed-and-breakfast in Little Haiti" but her determination has been vindicated by a stream of awards and guests happy to stay on the bank of the muddy Miami River, a ten-minute walk from Downtown Miami.

The compound of four wood frame buildings, with porches and screen doors, remind us of New England inns, except for the lofty palm trees by the swimming-pool. Simply labelled A, B, C and D, the houses were built between 1906 and 1910 to accommodate travellers on Henry Flagler's Florida East Coast railroad. Room A12, behind the reception desk, is typical, with a white rug on a natural wood floor, a brass bedstead with a floral spread, and white wicker furniture offsetting blue-painted, wood-panelled walls. Bathrooms are clean and bright.

This is a brisk, commercial operation, including 14 apartments for long stays. Breakfast is laid out for guests to help themselves. Iron gates and a tall fence provide security for guests and cars. Surprisingly, the neighbouring highway is little more than a hiss of traffic.

Nearby downtown Miami, Center for the Fine Arts, museum.

118 SW South River Drive, Miami, FL 33130
Tel (305) 325 0045; (800) 468 3589
Fax (305) 325 9227
Location directions essential; note that SW 4th Avenue is also called SW South River Drive. In residential area; own car parking
Meals breakfast
Prices rooms $-$$ with breakfast
Rooms 40 double; 38 have bath or shower, all have air-conditioning, phone, TV
Facilities breakfast-room; porches, garden, swimming-pool
Smoking restricted
Credit cards AE, DC, MC, V
Children very welcome
Disabled 3 adapted rooms
Closed never
Languages Spanish
Proprietor Sallye Jude

Greater Miami

Luxury hotel, South Miami Beach

Hotel Astor

Two blocks inland from Ocean Drive, the Astor is the first renovated hotel to open on Washington Avenue in years. While the exterior may resemble the original 60-year old building, the interior is "sort of New York cool," according to one of the first guests, late in 1995. Architecturally catalogued as Streamline rather than art deco, the original and rare painted Vitrolite glass has been proudly preserved in the foyer along with the original floor. Pale wood and pistachio green exemplify the restraint throughout, while attention to detail extends to soap, matchboxes and staff uniforms, all part of the design concept.

The resemblance to an ocean liner is emphasised by the contemporary tables, bedheads and desks, all hand-crafted by French woodworkers skilled in building luxury yachts. Clean-cut, plain and practical, they suit the neutral colour schemes which offer a real contrast to South Beach's often garish attempt at exciting decoration. The sophisticated luxury extends to the spa pool, with its fish mosaic, Jacuzzi jets and warbling water-sculpture. Local restaurant personality Dennis Max runs the 180-seat Astor Place which concentrates on new American cooking.

Nearby Art Deco District, beach, shopping.

956 Washington Avenue,
Miami Beach, FL 33139
Tel (305) 531 8081; (800) 270 4981
Fax (305) 531 3193
Location Washington Ave at 10th; public or valet car parking
Meals breakfast, lunch, dinner, snacks
Prices rooms $$-$$$$; charge for breakfast
Rooms 33 rooms, 9 suites; all have bath or shower, air-conditioning, phone, TV, minibar, hairdrier, safe
Facilities restaurant, sitting-room, bar, lift/elevator; patio
Smoking permitted
Credit cards AE, MC, V
Children over 12
Disabled 2 adapted rooms
Closed never
Languages French, German, Italian, Spanish
Manager Brian Safier

Greater Miami

Oceanfront hotel, South Miami Beach

Casa Grande

The man who gave the world Bob Marley, U2, Roxy Music and the Cranberries is now collecting hotels. Chris Blackwell, the founder of Island Records, has set up Island Outpost, a group of places to stay in Florida, the Bahamas and Jamaica. One of several on South Beach is Casa Grande, though it is not art deco architecture but rather two apartment blocks cleverly joined together by a wide, bright yellow hallway.

Although most of the building is condominiums, there are 33 hotel suites. Despite the heavily-carved teak and mahogany furniture and Indonesian batik fabrics, the rooms could be transplants from Manhattan, except for the ocean view from sitting-rooms. Otherwise, backgrounds are cool grey and burgundy, and there is a notable lack of clutter. Bathrooms are bold, however, with chunky green tiles on the floor and walls, as well as potted plants reflected in wall-to-wall mirrors.

The trendy Mezzaluna restaurant on the ground floor offers room service but many guests prefer to use the state-of-the-art kitchens where the night maid always leaves the coffee-maker ready for morning use. This is not for those on a budget.

Nearby Art Deco District, beach, shopping.

834 Ocean Drive, Miami Beach, FL 33139
Tel (305) 672 7003; (800) 688 7678
Fax (305) 673 3669
Location Ocean Drive between 8th and 9th Streets; public or valet car parking
Meals breakfast, lunch, dinner, snacks
Prices rooms $$$-$$$$; charge for breakfast
Rooms 38 suites; all have bath or shower, air-conditioning, phone, TV, VCR, radio, kitchen
Facilities lift/elevator, Mezzaluna restaurant
Smoking permitted
Credit cards AE, DC, MC, V
Children welcome
Disabled not suitable
Closed never
Languages Spanish, Swedish
Proprietors Island Outpost Hotels

Greater Miami

Idiosyncratic hotel, South Miami Beach

The Century

"People who come here know it's not the Holiday Inn," is the manager's assessment of one of South Beach's most eclectic hotels. It was rescued from decay by David Colby and Wilhelm Moser, arts enthusiasts and magazine publishers, who restored the 1940s art deco framework but gave Londoner Ron Arad a free hand with the interior. The result is either 'weird' or 'wonderful', depending on how avant-garde your aesthetics are.

The echoing reception area has sculptural metal furniture, with a lizard-shaped low table that echoes the hotel's logo. Copies of the owners' magazines spread on the terrazzo floor are anchored by a conch shell. Bedrooms are even more striking. One has deliberately-stained white sheets billowing at the windows; in another, black nylon drapes above a bed. Rooms are quite bare with, perhaps, a painting on an easel or a fax machine on a granite slab. With a model agency on site, the hotel is popular with fashion photographers, while the Century restaurant is open all hours. A 'New Age' breakfast is included in the price. More straightforward bedrooms are just across the street in the Beach Club which is right on the beach.

Nearby Art Deco District, beach, shopping, restaurants.

140 Ocean Drive, Miami Beach, FL 33139
Tel (305) 674 8855
Fax (305) 538 5733
Location at the southern end of Ocean Drive; limited car parking
Meals breakfast, lunch, dinner, snacks
Prices rooms $$-$$$$ with breakfast
Rooms 34 double; 12 suites; all have bath or shower, air-conditioning, phone, TV, VCR, beach towels; some faxes
Facilities restaurant, Lizard lounge; garden, patio
Smoking permitted
Credit cards AE, DC, MC, V
Children welcome
Disabled not suitable
Closed never
Languages French, German, Italian, Portuguese, Spanish
Proprietors David Colby and Wilhelm Moser

Greater Miami

Boutique hotel, South Miami Beach

Impala

Fashion magnate Gianni Versace could claim some credit for this hideaway in the heart of South Beach. When a Chicago-based design team were doing up his mansion, they could find no suitably stylish hotels nearby. So, in 1993, they transformed a 65-year old doss house into Miami's most exclusive boutique hotel which aims "to provide the service you'd expect in New York or Paris," according to owner Ken Lieber. The Café Impala restaurant is at the front, so guests follow a serpentine path through shrubbery to the entrance at the side.

In total contrast to the vibrancy of South Beach, the Impala is an oasis of restraint. Reception is in a small room with an eye-catching floor mosaic. The look throughout is sandy neutrals with wood, large potted plants and specially-made wrought iron work. Even the collages by another Chicagoan, artist James Faulkner, are low-key. A typical room has a pine sleigh bed with bright white sheets and goose down pillows. Bathrooms have large tubs or showers plus stainless steel wash-basins in coral rock surrounds. Verdict: a sophisticated version of a Tuscany villa where guests pay a premium for the privilege of privacy.

Nearby Art Deco District; beach, shopping.

1228 Collins Avenue, Miami Beach, FL 33139
Tel (305) 673 2021; (800) 646 7252
Fax (305) 673 5984
Location Collins Ave between 12th and 13th Streets; public or valet car parking
Meals breakfast, lunch, dinner, snacks
Prices rooms $$$$ with breakfast
Rooms 14 double; 3 suites; all have bath or shower, air-conditioning, phone, TV
Facilities Café Impala, lift/elevator
Smoking permitted
Credit cards AE, DC, MC, V
Children very welcome
Disabled 1 adapted room
Closed never; restaurant only, June to September
Languages French, German, Italian, Spanish
Proprietor Ken Lieber

Greater Miami

Historic hotel, South Miami Beach

Lafayette Hotel

Easy to spot, the large butter-cream and white building makes a refreshing alternative to the art deco style of many of its neighbours. A stone balustrade separates the sidewalk pavement from the small terrace where a cylindrical Parisian kiosk advertises local arts and entertainment. The European flavour continues throughout, reflecting the owners' Italian background.

When the 60-year old building was restored and redecorated in 1993, the entire Cattarossi family became involved, since the younger generation includes an engineer, two architects, one designer and a hotel manager. Italian influences are everywhere, from the private quarry-tiled patio with fountains to the elegant etchings on corridor walls and in the light, bright bedrooms. Even bathrooms have the cool grey and white tiling that is typically Italian-chic. At breakfast, the tastes of America and Europe merge into a copious buffet complete with crusty baguettes. South Beach is not really oriented to families with small children but the Cattarossis have cribs for babies. In Miami, the Lafayette is a rare and welcome combination of an up-market, comfortable hotel that is family-owned and run.

Nearby Art Deco District, beach, shopping.

944 Collins Avenue, Miami Beach, FL 33139
Tel (305) 673 2262
Fax (305) 534 5399
Location Collins Ave between 9th and 10th Streets; own car parking
Meals breakfast
Prices rooms $$$-$$$$ with breakfast
Rooms 20 double; 14 suites; all have bath or shower, air-conditioning, phone, TV, hairdrier, suites have CD players, minibar
Facilities dining-room, sitting area, bar, lift/elevator; patio
Smoking restricted
Credit cards AE, DC, MC, V
Children very welcome
Disabled suitable, 2 suites adapted
Closed never
Languages Chinese, French, German, Italian, Spanish
Proprietors Cattarossi family

Greater Miami

Celebrity hotel, South Miami Beach

The Marlin

Few hotels have a world-class recording studio in the basement but the owner of the squat, three-storey Marlin is Chris Blackwell (see Casa Grande p38). This was his first venture into the hospitality business and stars such as Prince, Bon Jovi, U2 and Cher have stayed in this unashamedly funky hotel, one block away from the ocean on Collins Avenue.

Reggae pounds out in the open-plan foyer, emphasising the Caribbean theme designed by Barbara Hulanicki of Biba fame from London's Swinging Sixties. Seashell lights on sea blue walls shine on the scallop-shaped bar. Beyond is a purple pool table. Corridors painted in rainbow colours lead to 12 exotic suites. The African Room has original naïve artwork from Cuba and Haiti, plus stencils of carrots, cabbages and tomatoes in the kitchenette. The Mexican Room vibrates with bold blues and yellows; the Barbie Room is sugar-candy pink. "Stars often shut the door, do their own cooking and listen to a new CD," says the manager. "They can even make a request on The Box, our affiliate music TV station across the street." For star-struck music fans, staying here could be a thrill, but not a cheap one.

Nearby Art Deco District, beach, shopping.

1200 Collins Avenue, Miami Beach, FL 33139
Tel (305) 673 8770; (800) 688 7678
Fax (305) 673 9609
Location corner of Collins and 12th Street; public or valet car parking
Meals breakfast, snacks
Prices rooms $$$$ with breakfast
Rooms 12 suites; all have bath or shower, air-conditioning, phone, TV, VCR, radio, hairdrier, kitchen, safe
Facilities bar, lift/elevator, recording studio; roof terrace
Smoking permitted
Credit cards AE, DC, MC, V
Children very welcome
Disabled not suitable
Closed never
Languages Spanish
Proprietors Island Outpost Hotels

Greater Miami

French hotel, South Miami Beach

Ocean Front

Bravado is needed to take on the Americans in their own back yard. That, however, is just what a young French husband-and-wife team has done, completely gutting twin 60-year old buildings and turning them into a luxury hotel-restaurant that is a small corner of the Côte d'Azur, complete with French newspapers and toiletries. 'Subdued, almost city-like,' reported our inspector, noting the quality fabrics and bedroom colour schemes such as champagne accented by deep blue or burgundy. Botanical fruit prints hang on walls, large vases of dried flowers recall Provence and art deco armoires conceal TV and VCR machines. Spacious, marble-tiled bathrooms reinforce the deep comfort.

On warm evenings, Les Deux Fontaines restaurant spills out of the brasserie on to the elevated terrace. Chef Jean-Pierre Petit's Mediterranean dishes have a North American accent: *ceviche* of grouper and snapper *provençale.*

The hotel is a fine vantage point for watching the sun and fun-seekers. When the noise level rises late at night, however, sound-proofed bedroom windows ensure a peaceful night's sleep. Not surprisingly, prices reflect the location and the luxury.

Nearby Art Deco District, beach, shopping.

1230-38 Ocean Drive, South Beach, FL 33139
Tel (305) 672 2579
Fax (305) 672 7665
Location between 11th and 12th Streets; public or valet car parking
Meals breakfast, lunch, dinner, snacks
Prices rooms $$$-$$$$ with breakfast
Rooms 27 double; all have bath or shower, air-conditioning, phone, TV, hairdrier; safe
Facilities 2 restaurants, lift/elevator; courtyard
Smoking permitted
Credit cards AE, DC, MC, V
Children welcome
Disabled 1 adapted room
Closed never
Languages French, Italian, Russian, Spanish
Managers Valerie and Xavier Lesmarie

Greater Miami

Idiosyncratic hotel, South Miami Beach

The Pelican

'Best stylistically exuberant hotel' was the vote of one local magazine in 1995 that obviously had no idea how to categorize the most eccentric of all South Beach's places to stay. When guests check in, the receptionist tries to match their personalities with the rooms available: 'Bang a Boomerang' or 'Some Like it Wet'? 'Me Tarzan, You Vain' or 'Do the Vehicle'?

The hotel is owned by the Diesel Jeans company, known for its bizarre advertising. They allowed Swedish designer Magnus Ehrland total freedom to express his version of the American Dream. Some may rate the result the American Nightmare. Recycling is a theme throughout. One bedroom has sheet metal bolted to walls, another a wood floor saved from a church in North Carolina. Mattresses, however, are new while shower-heads are 'real drenchers'. Located halfway along Ocean Drive, the ambience is high-energy, youthful and self-consciously trendy. Ford's world-famous model agency has an office here, so photography teams plus stars of the music and fashion worlds book in. We decided it was an amusing, if rather expensive, experience. Not a place for a relaxing holiday.

Nearby Art Deco District, beach, shopping.

826 Ocean Drive, Miami Beach, FL 33139
Tel (305) 673 3373; (800) 7 PELICAN
Fax (305) 673 3255
Location on Ocean Drive between 8th and 9th Streets; public or valet car parking
Meals breakfast, lunch, dinner
Prices rooms $$$-$$$$ with breakfast
Rooms 22 double; 4 suites; all have bath or shower, air-conditioning, phone, TV, VCR, radio, refrigerator, safe; 1 with Jacuzzi
Facilities Pelican restaurant, bar, lift/elevator
Smoking permitted
Credit cards AE, DC, MC, V
Children welcome
Disabled 1 adapted room
Closed never
Languages Italian, Spanish
Manager Massimo Furlan

Greater Miami

Beach hotel, South Miami Beach

La Voile Rouge Hotel & Beach Club

South Beach is a casual place, particularly when it comes to dress. One exception is this European-style beach club where a sign dictates 'proper attire required'. Privacy is ensured by the uniformed security guard who screens members, hotel-guests and those with reservations at the in-house restaurant, the 12th in the international Bice Ristorante group.

It is hard to believe that the two-storey building was derelict when the Wang brothers bought it in the early 1990s. Now, the eight spacious bedrooms are studies in no-expense-spared interior design; those we saw are more minimalist than plush, with plain walls and tiled floors. Each has an exotic theme. In 'Santa Fe', for example, a cattle skull with horns and clever *trompe l'oeil* mural reinforce the New Mexico look.

One of the most expensive hotels in this book, La Voile Rouge trades on its St Tropez-style exclusivity as much as its position directly on the beach. With both a shallow and a deeper pool in the garden, guests have no need to mix with the public when swimming. With a strong European clientele, smoking is not only permitted, it is the focus of the dark wood-panelled Cigar Bar.
Nearby Art Deco District, beach, shopping.

455 Ocean Drive, Miami Beach, FL 33139
Tel (305) 535 0099; (800) LA VOILE
Fax (305) 532 4442
Location Ocean Drive between 4th and 5th Streets; valet or public car parking
Meals breakfast, lunch, dinner, snacks
Prices rooms $$$$ breakfast
Rooms 8 double; 2 suites; all have bath or shower, air-conditioning, phone, TV, radio, minibar, hairdrier; safe
Facilities restaurant, bar, sauna and fitness area; terrace, 2 swimming-pools
Smoking permitted
Credit cards AE, MC, V
Children welcome
Disabled not suitable
Closed never; restaurant only, Mon lunch **Languages** French, Spanish; some German
Proprietor Cliff Wang

More on page 145

The Keys

Luxury inn, Key West

The Gardens Hotel

Every inn in Key West has a lush garden but this one is exceptional. "It's like waking up in Kew Gardens," said one guest from London. For 50 years, this was the private estate of Peggy Mills, a local legend and self-taught gardener, who slowly transformed an unkempt, weed-covered plot into one of the best-known botanic gardens in the entire state. In the unusually spacious grounds are mango, balsa and breadfruit trees, eight varieties of palms and a kaleidoscope of tropical flowers.

When Bill and Corinna Hettinger bought the property in 1992, they had to restore the landscaping, abandoned after Mrs Mills' death. They also decided to convert her home into a light, airy hotel that would match the extraordinary setting. Instead of run-of-the-mill wicker or dark Victorian antiques, they hung fine chintz curtains, painted walls white, restored the original floors and added specially-made yew cabinets.

Do not be deceived by the apparent simplicity: this is one of the best examples we have seen anywhere of the art of understated luxury. Arguably the 'best place in town', it is also the most expensive, but, then, staying here feels almost like a privilege.

Nearby beach, restaurants, shopping, water sports.

526 Angela Street, Key West, FL 33040
Tel (305) 294 2661; (800) 526 2664; in the UK, (0800) 964 470
Fax (305) 292 1007
Location corner of Angela and Simonton Streets; ample car parking
Meals breakfast
Prices rooms $$$$ with breakfast
Rooms 17 double; 1 suite; 1 cottage; all have bath or shower, air-conditioning, phone, TV, radio, minibar, hairdrier; safe
Facilities 2 sitting-rooms; bar, terrace, garden, swimming-pool **Smoking** permitted
Credit cards AE, MC, V
Children welcome
Disabled access to 1 room
Closed never **Languages** French, Italian, Spanish
Manager Evelyn Baskin

The Keys

Bed-and-breakfast, Key West

Heron House

After listening to pop songs thumping out of the stores and cafés along Duval Street, the classical music playing in the garden of the Heron House soothes the sensibilities. Plants are easy to grow in Key West's near-tropical climate, but here the gardens look particularly exotic because the speciality is orchids. There are hundreds of different types from Hawaii, Asia and the Caribbean. They hang from branches and dangle from trellises. Some are bold and splashy, others tiny and delicate. Not content with these glamourous epiphytes, Fred Geibelt's latest project is to create his own mini-rain forest.

You don't have to be a keen botanist, however, to enjoy staying here. This is one of the larger inns in town, so there is no enforced chumminess. Staff are helpful but low-key, in contrast to the extroverts we found elsewhere. In the morning, they set out breakfast under the huge gumbo limbo, one of the few trees native to the Keys. Guests eat here, on their balconies or by the swimming-pool. Basic rooms tend to be small, with a shower and WC but the higher-priced rooms are stylish, with unusual walls of inlaid oak, mahogany, and rosewood and baths set in granite.
Nearby beach, restaurants, shopping, water sports.

512 Simonton Street, Key West, FL 33040
Tel (305) 294 9227
Fax (305) 294 5692
Location between Fleming St and Southard St; public car parking on street
Meals breakfast
Prices rooms $$-$$$$ breakfast
Rooms 23 double; all have bath or shower, air-conditioning, phone, TV, radio; some hairdrier
Facilities decks, garden, heated swimming-pool
Smoking permitted
Credit cards AE, MC, V
Children not suitable
Disabled not suitable
Closed never
Languages English only
Proprietor Fred Geibelt

The Keys

Garden hotel, Key West

Island City House Hotel

In Key West, small may be beautiful but it can also be a little cramped, so the spaciousness of this complex sets it apart from most of the other inns. The L-shaped garden is big enough for a breeze to circulate under the tall palms, even in the sultriest weather. There are chairs and fountains shaded by avocado and Spanish lime trees, plus a larger-than-usual swimming-pool. Best of all, guests here do not have the feeling of being overlooked.

The hotel consists of three buildings, set well apart from each other in the grounds. The Island City House, built in 1889, has the delicate tiers of verandas typical of Southern and Caribbean architecture. The old carriage house, the last of its kind in Key West, has been converted into six rooms, while the Cigar House is new, a reproduction of an old Key West cigar factory.

The entire place has been renovated by architects Stan and Jan Corneal, who moved down from Philadelphia to take over the family business in 1992. Since they have children of their own, they were determined to create an hotel large enough to accommodate couples as well as families. In this town, that is an unusual combination; happily, they have succeeded.

Nearby beach, restaurants, shopping, water sports.

411 William Street, Key West, FL 33040
Tel (305) 294 5702; (800) 634 8230
Fax (305) 294 1289
Location on William St and Eaton St; public car parking on street
Meals breakfast
Prices rooms $$-$$$$ with breakfast
Rooms 24 suites; all have bath or shower, Jacuzzi, air-conditioning, phone, TV, radio, refrigerator
Facilities terrace, garden, swimming-pool
Smoking permitted restricted outdoors only
Credit cards DC, MC, V
Children very welcome
Disabled not suitable
Closed never
Languages English only
Proprietors Jan and Stan Corneal

The Keys

Bed-and-breakfast, Key West

Key West Bed & Breakfast

Jody Carlson chose the inn's subtitle, The Popular House, "because it is a Caribbean term for a place that you put all your time, money and energy into and is very colourful." Jody, a painter and weaver, is one of a stream of artists and writers who have settled in Key West after John Dos Passos and Ernest Hemingway gave it cachet in the 1930s. Some of the paintings on the walls are her own work, she bought others while living in the West Indies. All have bold, dramatic colours. Her loom stands in the sitting-room where rainbow-hued skeins of wool line the shelves. The overall effect is part art gallery, part private home.

It was artisans rather than artists, however, that built the house. They were boat-builders from the Bahamas, which is supposed to explain the slight rocking sensation felt when high winds blow. Some bedrooms are small, though in the attic, the two Treehouse Rooms are larger, with windows facing sunrise or sunset.

We like the contemporary look of this inn, which makes a welcome change from the dark Victorian or 'wicker and rattan' styles found throughout Key West. On the other hand, only half the rooms have private baths and the garden is rather small.

Nearby beach, restaurants, shopping, water sports.

415 William Street, Key West, FL 33040
Tel (305) 296 7274; (800) 438 6155
Location between Eaton St and Fleming St; public car parking on street
Meals breakfast
Prices rooms $-$$$$ with breakfast
Rooms 7 double; 1 single; 4 have bath or shower, air-conditioning
Facilities sitting-room; terrace, garden, hot tub
Smoking restricted
Credit cards AE, DC, MC, V
Children over 13
Disabled not suitable
Closed never
Languages English only
Proprietor Jody Carlson

Historic mansion, Key West

Lightbourn Inn

During Fantasy Fest, the week-long October carnival, parades of costumed revellers wind through the Old Town. Once a gay celebration, it now attracts a wider audience, with groups of friends and straight couples all joining in the fun. Each year, a King of the festival is elected. Foxton was entered but he didn't win, though he had the backing of celebrities, who sent him their photographs and best wishes. Those pictures hang in the hall of Foxton's home, the Lightbourn Inn.

Foxton is a fox terrier whose owners, Kelly Summers and Scott Fuhriman, proprietors of the Lightbourn Inn, are party-lovers. Their collection of fancy-dress hats in the old dining-room could kit out an entire pageant. They also amass teddy bears and unusual antiques, such as an elaborate gold Chinese screen. In contrast to these displays, the rest of the inn looks surprisingly plain, straightforward and uncluttered. Some bedrooms are in the main house, others are in two smaller buildings at the back, beside the swimming-pool.

Do remember that its 'all welcome' philosophy means that the clientele could be a mixture of gay and straight visitors.

Nearby beach, restaurants, shopping, water sports.

907 Truman Avenue, Key West, FL 33040
Tel (305) 296 5152; (800) 352 6011
Fax (305) 294 9490
Location two blocks from Duval Street; own car parking
Meals breakfast
Prices rooms $$-$$$$ with breakfast
Rooms 10 double; all have bath or shower, air-conditioning, phone, TV; some radio
Facilities sitting-room; terrace, decks, swimming-pool
Smoking outdoors only
Credit cards AE, DC, MC, V
Children not suitable
Disabled access to 1 room
Closed never
Languages German, Chinese
Proprietors Kelly Summers, Scott Fuhriman

The Keys

Luxury hotel, Key West

The Marquesa

In Key West, every other house seems to be a bed-and-breakfast or a guest-house. The Marquesa is one of the few exceptions. This is a small, professionally-staffed, luxury hotel-and-restaurant of the sort found all over Europe. Most visitors strolling through the heart of the Old Town spot the Café Marquesa first and stop to peer in at the whimsical painting of a kitchen on the back wall. Chef Todd has a high reputation for his 'food of the Americas', which translates into dishes such as spicy prawns with grilled pineapple, papaya and black bean relish.

Next door, the hotel shows the hand of an interior designer rather than the personal mementoes of an innkeeper. Chairs and tables are carefully matched, flowers in tall vases are deliberately arranged. The quality is obvious, but to feel the spirit, step into the garden at the back. This feels like a little village with cottage-like porches opening on to two swimming-pools and the usual array of tropical flowers and palms.

This may not be the funky Key West of the guidebooks but many relish the deep comfort and tranquillity. One black mark: at their prices, why do they have to charge for breakfast?

Nearby beach, restaurants, shopping, water sports.

600 Fleming St, Key West, FL 33040
Tel (305) 292 1919; (800) 869 4631
Fax (305) 294 2121
Location corner of Fleming St and Simonton St; own car parking
Meals breakfast
Prices rooms $$$-$$$$; charge for breakfast
Rooms 25 double; 2 suites; all have bath or shower, air-conditioning, phone, TV, radio, safe; some hairdrier
Facilities sitting-room; terrace, garden, 2 swimming-pools
Smoking permitted
Credit cards AE, DC, MC, V
Children welcome
Disabled 1 adapted room
Closed never
Languages French, Spanish
Proprietor Carol Wightman

The Keys

Beach-side inn, Key West

La Mer Hotel and Dewey House

With its array of art galleries and boutiques, its tours of famous homes and gardens, it is easy to forget that Key West is also attractive for beach holidays. Of all the inns we recommend in town, this is the only one right on the water. Washed by the Atlantic, City Beach is small and open to the public. Since access is not easy, it is less crowded than better-known stretches of sand, such as the nearby Southernmost Beach at the bottom of Duval Street. At La Mer and the Dewey House, guests can roll out of bed and be in the sea in seconds.

In fact, La Mer and the Dewey House would be attractive whatever their location. Neither funky nor family-oriented, these two 19thC houses 'offer privacy with the comforts of a four-star hotel,' according to our inspector, who was impressed by The Dewey House, opened in late 1995. Rooms here are opulent in green and gold, with large bathrooms. La Mer is more straightforward, with tropical prints and toning plain colours. Although rooms with an ocean view are booked well in advance, most of the others have private porches looking on to gardens, and the beach is still only a few steps away.

Nearby beach, restaurants, shopping, water sports.

506 South Street, Key West, FL 33040
Tel (305) 296 5611; (800) 354 4455
Fax (305) 294 8272
Location off Duval Street; ample car parking
Meals breakfast, afternoon snacks
Prices rooms $$-$$$$ with breakfast
Rooms 19 double; all have bath or shower, air-conditioning, phone, TV, radio, hairdrier, minibar, safe
Facilities sitting-room; porches, Jacuzzi, swimming-pools
Smoking permitted
Credit cards AE, MC, V
Children not suitable
Disabled not suitable
Closed never
Languages English only
Managers Carrie and Matt Babich

The Keys

Bed-and-breakfast, Key West

The Merlinn

When social-worker Pat Hoffman decided on a career change a decade ago, she chose Key West for its "blue skies and interesting people." Instead of restoring an historic building, however, she renovated a 1940s-built boarding-house and created an oasis of calm, with the emphasis on informality.

Every inn has its regulars; here, they seem to be the sort of people who read hard-back books and enjoy lively conversation. This could be because, unlike many bed-and-breakfasts in town, there is a sitting-room indoors.

The outdoors is different, too. Where so many gardens here feel hemmed in due to the density of tropical plants, hers looks lighter and more open, with wooden decks, a Japanese-style wooden bridge by the swimming-pool and two huge maho trees for shade. It is, however, on the street-side rather than behind the inn.

Bedrooms in the main house and cottages vary in size and price; we found them attractive and comfortable but not plush. One of the most stylish is the Tea House suite, adapted for wheelchairs, with a second bedroom up a spiral staircase for a companion. As well as several cats, Pat keeps exotic caged birds.

Nearby beach, restaurants, shopping, water sports.

811 Simonton Street, Key West, FL 33040
Tel (305) 296 3336
Fax (305) 296 3524
Location corner of Simonton St and Petronia St; public car parking on street
Meals breakfast
Prices rooms $-$$$ with breakfast
Rooms 11 double; 2 suites; 5 cottages; all have bath or shower, air-conditioning, TV
Facilities sitting-room; decks, garden, heated swimming-pool **Smoking** outdoors only
Credit cards AE, MC, V
Children welcome
Disabled 1 adapted cottage
Closed never
Languages English only
Proprietor Pat Hoffman

The Keys

Bed-and-breakfast complex, Key West

The Paradise Inn

Key West inns have long had a reputation for being laid-back and casual, but there have been changes in recent years. Atmosphere is no longer enough; more affluent visitors are happy to come, as long as they can stay in greater comfort. So, inns are expanding, remodelling and redecorating, while brand new places, such as the Paradise Inn, are opening at the luxury end of the scale.

When Shel Segel, a florist, joined forces with George Pentz, owner of the White Street Inn (see p153), they started from scratch. Using Shel's former flower shop, several nearby cottages, and even some new but traditionally-styled houses, they turned a cluster of buildings into an inn. They commissioned an award-winning landscape architect to design the gardens with unusual plants such as the ylang-ylang, whose yellow blooms perfume the air with a scent rather like Chanel Number 5.

Finally, they filled bedrooms with plenty of creature comforts. The neutral decoration lacks the individuality of other inns, but some may find it a refreshing change from themed decoration and collections of treasures. Overall, the Paradise, which opened at the end of 1995, is a welcome addition to the Key West scene.
Nearby beach, restaurants, shopping, water sports.

819 Simonton Street, Key West, FL 33040
Tel (305) 293 8007; (800) 888 9648
Fax (305) 293 0807
Location between Olivia St and Petronia St; own car parking
Meals breakfast
Prices rooms $$$-$$$$ with breakfast
Rooms 8 double; 7 suites; 3 cottages; all have bath or shower, air-conditioning, phone, TV, radio, minibar, hairdrier, safe
Facilities breakfast-room; garden, swimming-pool
Smoking permitted
Credit cards AE, DC, MC, V
Children welcome
Disabled 1 adapted room
Closed never
Languages some German
Proprietors Shel Segel, George Pentz

The Keys

Historic inn, Key West

Pilot House

The Pilot House started out in 1990 as a typical Key West bed-and-breakfast. Soon, however, owner Ed Cox learned that his guests did not care about having the personal touch of an innkeeper. They didn't even care about breakfast. What they wanted most was to be left to their own devices. So, he moved the office into a building separate from the rest of the inn and stopped serving food. He did, however, put cooking facilities into the rooms, so guests have the choice of making their own breakfast or strolling around the corner to one of the numerous restaurants and cafés along Duval Street.

Although this goes against the philosophy of this book, we include the Pilot House because it is comfortable, convenient and above all, private. Some guests choose the Victorian atmosphere of the Julius Otto House, the original inn with creaky floors and squeaky doors. Others prefer the contemporary look of the Poolside Cabana, which opened in 1995.

The Pilot House is an 'all welcome' place and there might be nude sunbathing by the swimming-pool. Anyone who finds this offensive should book a room elsewhere.

Nearby beach, restaurants, shopping, water sports.

414 Simonton Street, Key West, FL 33040
Tel (305) 294 8719; (800) 648 3780
Fax (305) 294 9298
Location on Simonton and Eaton Streets; public car parking
Meals no meals served
Prices rooms $$-$$$$
Rooms 16 double; 4 suites; all have bath or shower, air-conditioning, phone, TV, radio, refrigerator
Facilities outdoor Jacuzzi, swimming-pool
Smoking restricted
Credit cards AE, DC, MC, V
Children not suitable
Disabled 1 adapted room
Closed never
Languages English only
Proprietor Ed Cox

The Keys

Historic inn, Key West

Simonton Court

A century ago, Cuban immigrants developed cigar-making into a major industry in Key West. Simonton Court was one of several factories where the owner, foreman and labourers all lived and worked together on the compound. Now, the tang of tobacco has been replaced by the scent of exotic flowers in the lush gardens, while nine buildings, scattered around the large L-shaped lot, offer guests a choice both of style and atmosphere.

Standing right on Simonton Street, two houses, called the Inn and the Manor House, protect the privacy of the rest of the hotel. An old red-brick alley cuts between them, leading past six tin-roofed cottages, with porches and white wicker furniture. Built for the workers' families, they are large enough for two couples. Tucked into the corner of the grounds is the former owner's home, the Mansion, with its authentic but rather sombre Victorian furniture. The Bird of Paradise suite, however, has access to a widow's walk with roof-top views of the water.

Stylish and comfortable, Simonton Court is for adults only. Where most inns have one swimming-pool, here there are four, including one painted black, with 'sensual lighting' at night.
Nearby beach, restaurants, shopping, water sports.

320 Simonton Street, Key West, FL 33040
Tel (305) 294 6386; (800) 944 2687
Fax (305) 293 8446
Location between Eaton St and Caroline St; limited car parking, daily charge
Meals breakfast
Prices rooms $$-$$$$ with breakfast
Rooms 13 double; 7 suites; 6 cottages; all have bath or shower, air-conditioning, phone, TV, radio, refrigerator; most have hairdrier, kitchenette; 3 Jacuzzi
Facilities terrace, garden, 4 swimming-pools
Smoking permitted
Credit cards AE, MC, V
Children not suitable
Disabled not suitable
Closed never
Languages English only
Manager Greg Kidwell

The Keys

Luxury resort, Little Torch Key

Little Palm Island

Aficionados consider this destination to be the ultimate Florida hideaway: a private island three miles (4.5 km) offshore and accessible only by boat or seaplane. The complex of buildings includes 14 cottages whose South Seas-style roofs, thatched in palm, rustle in the evening breeze. Each houses two suites where decoration combines elegance with island simplicity. A swathe of white muslin drapes from a beam over the bed but bathrooms have Mexican tiles instead of white marble. Rooms are smaller than in deluxe city hotels, but then guests probably spend most of their time outdoors. Chef Michel Reymond's menus, however, read like a big-city restaurant, with a wine list to match.

With orchids and allspice, green herons and hummingbirds, the lush grounds feel like a quiet nature reserve. Jet skis are not allowed and morning papers are delivered by golf carts. Guests sunbathe on the sandy beach and swim in the pool, or use the canoes, sailboats and snorkel gear, which are included in the admittedly high prices. Although staff outnumber guests by nearly two-to-one, service is friendly rather than obsequious. For a special experience, this is difficult to match.

Nearby wildlife sanctuary, water sports, beach.

Route 4, Box 1036, Little Torch Key, FL 33042
Tel (305) 872 2524; (800) 343 8567; in UK (0800) 964 470
Fax (305) 872 4843
Location MM 28.5 Overseas Highway US 1; ample car parking at shore station
Meals breakfast, lunch, dinner, snacks
Prices rooms $$$$
Rooms 30 suites; all have whirpool bath, shower, air-conditioning, minibar, deck
Facilities dining-room, bar, sauna and fitness area; terrace, garden, swimming-pool, beach, boats
Smoking permitted
Credit cards AE, DC, MC, V
Children over 12
Disabled 1 adapted room
Closed never
Languages French
Managing General Partner Ben H Woodson

More on page 148

Southwest

Gulfside resort, Englewood

Manasota Beach Club

One of a handful of small inns that can truthfully boast of being right on the beach, this is a one-off, a low-key resort where families return year after year, to meet up with friends and unite the generations. They canoe and sail, fish and swim, play tennis and croquet, hunt for fossils and spot some of the 93 species of birds on the key. Since these activities, as well as three meals a day, are included in the rate, we think prices are reasonable.

Yet the club is a well-kept secret, set on Englewood Key, one of the barrier islands that parallel the Gulf Coast. Some ten miles (16 km) north of Venice, it is a wildlife preserve, though there are private houses set back from the quiet main road.

The Buffum family, hoteliers from Rhode Island, bought the club in 1960 making improvements but keeping the natural look. In the spacious grounds, sea grape and tall Australian pines grow wild between cottages which are homey and comfortable rather than decorator-designed. We like the old-fashioned ambience that reminds us of an informal country club, right down to the 'jacket and tie' rule for dinner. Unfortunately, the main season is short, just four months from winter into spring.

Nearby golf, Sarasota.

7660 Manasota Key Road, Englewood, FL 34223
Tel (941) 474 2614
Fax (941) 473 1512
Location secluded estate on the Gulf; ample car parking
Meals breakfast, lunch, dinner
Prices rooms $$$$ including breakfast, lunch, dinner
Rooms 12 double; 3 single; 7 suites; 8 cottages; all have bath or shower; some air-conditioning, phone, kitchens
Facilities 3 dining-rooms, 2 sitting-rooms; garden, swimming-pool, tennis courts
Smoking permitted restricted outdoors only
Credit cards not accepted
Children very welcome
Disabled not suitable
Closed June to Nov; dining-room closed, Dec, May
Languages English only
Proprietors Buffum family

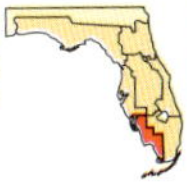

Southwest

Beach inn, Ft Myers at Sanibel

Song of the Sea

Sanibel is famous for the Sanibel Stoop, the hunched position adopted by visitors as they search for shells on one of the best-known beaches in the USA. Waves that sweep round the Gulf of Mexico drop huge quantities of shells on to the soft white sand. The seemingly infinite varieties and colours are a constant source of pleasure to young and old: they stoop at dawn, high noon and dusk, yet however many are toted off in buckets and boxes, there are always more to collect the next day.

Thousands flock to stay in the private homes and condominiums on the island, but few have the privilege of holidaying right on the beach. That is why Song of the Sea is so popular. The trio of low blocks may be plain and practical, but they are ideal for families, since small children can play on the large lawns, use the big swimming-pool and run on to the sand to pick up shells.

Totally renovated in 1991, rooms have pretty fabrics, firm mattresses and modern furniture. Although there are kitchens, a help-yourself breakfast is set out in reception. The straightforward comfort suits vacationers from Europe and the USA. Prices may seem high, but everyone pays a premium to stay on Sanibel.

Nearby restaurants, shopping, water sports.

863 East Gulf Drive, Sanibel Island, FL 33957
Tel (941) 472 2220; (800) 231 1045; in Europe (44) 181 367 5175
Fax (941) 481 4947
Location on south shore, not far from causeway; car parking
Meals breakfast
Prices rooms $$$-$$$$ with breakfast
Rooms 22 double; 8 suites; all have bath or shower, Jacuzzi, air-conditioning, phone, TV, VCR, radio, hairdrier, kitchen, safe
Facilities reception area; garden, swimming-pool
Smoking permitted
Credit cards AE, DC, MC, V
Children very welcome
Disabled not suitable
Closed never
Languages English only
Manager Brenda Geiger

More on page 157

Southeast

Bed-and-breakfast, Lauderdale-by-the-Sea

A Little Inn by the Sea

Halfway between Palm Beach and Miami, the inn is in a seemingly never-ending row of hotels built for northern 'snowbirds' who want nothing more than sun, sand and surf. Although it backs on to busy Route A1A, the front is right on the beach.

The 29-room size fulfils the 'small' requirement; the 'charm' is provided by the Brandt family from Switzerland. Although the European tradition of hotel-keeping shows here, they remain in tune with their surroundings. "It's the kind of place where it's OK to track in some sand," says one guest. Overall, we give this a high rating for beach holidays, particularly for families who have young children.

A selection of foreign newspapers proves that Europeans are regular visitors. Although the two-storey high atrium doubles as breakfast-room and reception, the focus is the courtyard swimming-pool where palm trees provide protection from sun and wind. The ever-present Florida motifs of fish and shells abound, but the quality of fabrics and wicker furniture is high, and the Brandts are constantly upgrading. Room 212 has the best views up and down the long stretch of tempting beach.

Nearby Pompano race track, golf, restaurants.

4546 El Mar Drive, Lauderdale-by-the-Sea, FL 33308
Tel (954) 772 2450; (800) 492 0311
Fax (954) 938 9354
Location rte A1A between Atlantic and Commercial Blvds; ample car parking
Meals breakfast
Prices rooms $-$$$$ with breakfast
Rooms 29 double; all have bath or shower, air-conditioning, phone, TV,
Facilities heated swimming-pool, bicycles, tennis-courts
Smoking permitted
Credit cards AE, DC, MC, V
Children very welcome
Disabled not suitable
Closed never
Languages French, German
Proprietors Ulrich Brandt and family

Southeast

Bed-and-breakfast hotel, Palm Beach

Plaza Inn

Other than in Miami, we do not include many hotels of this size. Nevertheless, we feel that Ajit Asrani, a former Indian Army officer and a real character, deserves an A for effort. On one of Palm Beach's busier and less lovely streets, the plain 1930s exterior gives no clue to the interior, ambitiously aiming at European grandeur. For a start, Mr Asrani greets visitors wearing a suit and tie. This formality may not appeal to those more comfortable in shorts and sandals, but the Plaza trades more on privacy and service than sun and sand.

The reception desk echoes the Louis XV style, chandeliers hang from moulded, gilded ceilings, while antiques and a baby grand piano continue the conceit. With its dark wood and striped walls, the Stray Fox pub copies the old-fashioned look of a bar in a British gentlemen's club.

All 50 bedrooms are individually decorated. Number 208 has a black-and-gold art deco theme, while Number 201 feels more like New England, with a sleigh bed and armoire. If there is a disappointment, it is the site of the swimming-pool and outdoor hot tub, wedged between the sidewalk and the parking lot.

Nearby Royal Palm Way, Worth Avenue shopping, polo, golf.

215 Brazilian Avenue, Palm Beach, FL 33480
Tel (407) 832 8666; (800) 233 2632
Fax (407) 835 8776
Location between Hibiscus and South County Rd; ample car parking
Meals breakfast
Prices rooms $$-$$$$ with breakfast
Rooms 50 double; all have bath or shower, air-conditioning, phone, TV, radio, refrigerator
Facilities dining-room, sitting-room, bar, lift/elevator; heated swimming-pool, hot tub
Smoking permitted
Credit cards AE, DC, MC, V
Children welcome
Disabled not suitable
Closed never
Languages English only
Proprietor Ajit Asrani

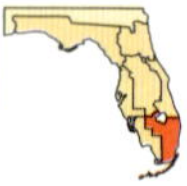

Southeast

Beach hotel, Palm Beach

Sea Lord Hotel

Palm Beach Island's strip of ocean-side real estate is among the world's most exclusive and desirable. The stretch on Route A1A lying between the Atlantic Ocean and the Intracoastal Waterway is a roll call of spectacular private mansions and grand hotels such as the legendary 500-room Breakers. No wonder it has been nicknamed the Gold Coast. The rich and famous can swim in the sea here, because there are few spots with public parking, let alone public access. In the midst of all this opulence, the Sea Lord stands out for being unpretentious and well-priced.

The hotel has a traditional beach front façade of bright white and aqua colours, punctuated by glass bricks. Inside, there are no frills. Communal rooms are plain, bedrooms are merely comfortable, with modern bathrooms. Those in the South Wing are smaller and cheaper than rooms with ocean views. If the inn is full, guests stay in the Chalet on the Intracoastal Waterway.

This is ideal for families and couples who want a glimpse of the glamour of Palm Beach at affordable prices. Even the pool-side café concentrates on simple food, since numerous smart restaurants are within walking distance.

Nearby Flagler Museum, golf, Lion Country Safari.

2315 South Ocean Boulevard, Palm Beach, FL 33480
Tel (407) 582 1461; (800) 638 6217
Location off Rte A1A in heart of Palm Beach; ample car parking
Meals breakfast, lunch, dinner
Prices rooms $-$$$ with breakfast
Rooms 40 double; all have bath or shower, air-conditioning, phone, TV, refrigerator; some kitchenettes
Facilities dining-room, sitting-room, lift/elevator; heated swimming-pool
Smoking permitted
Credit cards AE, MC, V
Children welcome
Disabled not suitable
Closed never
Languages English only
Proprietors Bob Hardy

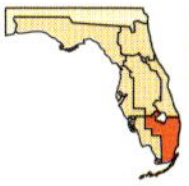

Southeast

Waterside home, Palm Beach Gardens

Heron Cay

Guests who stay here can start the day by zooming down a slide into the deep swimming-pool from the wrap-around balcony right outside their bedrooms. This touch of frivolity typifies the style of Randy Burgener and Margie Salyer whose home is filled with their collections of juke boxes, pinball machines and pub paraphernalia. Beyond the pool are private boat slips, the Intracoastal Waterway and a floating dock leading to their own mangrove island which feels like a nature reserve, complete with a trail to a sandy beach. We did not expect to find all this in what, from the street, looks like an ordinary residential area.

Since 1990, Heron Cay has become a popular getaway spot for locals. Some arrive by boat, turning off the Intracoastal Waterway at marker 23; others come by car, passing the dinghy and sea-faring flotsam marooned on the grass at the front. Bedrooms vary in size; bathrooms are generous. With a commercial-grade kitchen, breakfasts can be adventurous.

We like the down-to-earth attitudes and infectious humour of the owners of this idiosyncratic, two-storey house. Staying here could provide entertaining memories for years to come.

Nearby Palm Beach, shopping, golf, Intracoastal Waterway.

15106 Palmwood Road, Palm Beach Gardens, FL 33410
Tel (407) 744 6315
Fax (407) 744 0943
Location in quiet residential area; ample car parking
Meals breakfast
Prices rooms $$-$$$ with breakfast
Rooms 6 double; all have bath or shower, air-conditioning; 1 with TV, 5 with refrigerators
Facilities deck, swimming-pool, hot tub, dockage, island
Smoking permitted
Credit cards MC, V
Children over 6
Disabled not suitable
Closed never
Languages English only
Proprietors Randy Burgener, Margie Salyer

Southeast

Waterside inn, Stuart

HarborFront Inn

Stuart grew up on the mainland where the St Lucie River crosses the Indian River Intracoastal Waterway. Back in 1908, when the house was built, access was by footpath or by water. Some guests still arrive by boat and boats are the focus of this inn. Owner John Elbert is a sea captain and will take guests fishing and sailing, but there are also a kayak and a small powerboat for hire. Since Stuart calls itself the 'sailfish capital of the world' and attracts many fishermen, the breakfast buffet is ready at 7.30 am so boaters can be off early. A hot dish, however, is offered from 8.30-9.00 am for later-risers. Picnic lunches can be provided.

The architecture is 'fascinating, like a Nantucket shingled cottage but with Florida woods' such as cypress and southern pine. Works by local artists plus plenty of wicker and rattan add up to an informal beach-house feeling and although the inn caters to nautical types, each room has its own entrance, so the sense of privacy would suit those wanting to get away from it all.

Lawns, with palm and fruit trees, stretch down to the river where landlubbers may enjoy the dockside activity from the safety of the double hammock, just a stone's throw from the water.

Nearby restored downtown; golf; beaches 5 m (8 km) away.

310 Atlanta Avenue, Stuart, FL 34994
Tel (407) 288 7289; (800) 294 1703
Fax (407) 221 0474
Location on St Lucie River; ample car parking
Meals breakfast
Prices rooms $-$$$ with breakfast
Rooms 4 double; 1 suite; 1 apartment; 1 cottage; all have bath or shower, air-conditioning, TV, radio, hairdrier
Facilities dining-room, sitting-room; patio, garden, dockage, boats **Smoking** outdoors only
Credit cards AE, MC, V
Children over 12
Disabled not suitable
Closed first week in June, last 2 weeks Sept
Languages English only
Proprietors JoAyne and John Elbert

Southeast

Town bed-and-breakfast, Stuart

The Homeplace

Follow Stuart's Historic Walking Tour and Sam Matthews becomes a familiar name. A builder from Massachusetts, he came to Stuart when it was a community of pineapple plantations and was a key figure in its early development. The Homeplace was Matthews' own home, built in 1913. From here, the small historic district and waterfront are just a short walk away.

Restored in 1989, the house retains a Victorian feel with love seats and steamer trunks among other antiques. Step inside and you can see past the dining-room and sun porch to the garden where grapefruit, orange and banana trees produce fruit for breakast. Bedrooms may be on the small side but are more windows than walls for maximum ventilation. The Captain's Room, in burgundy, gold and black, has a ship's figure-head, a busty painted lady, while Opal's Room is named for the local girl whose bedside diary describes turn-of-the-century life. This homey, informal hideaway is popular with couples from Tampa and Ft Lauderdale. Some fish, play golf and go to the beach only 5 miles (8 km) away; others do nothing but sunbathe and swim in the pool, which is large enough for exercise.

Nearby fishing, golf, beaches; Historic District.

501 Akron Avenue, Stuart, FL 34994
Tel (407) 220 9148
Location in old area of downtown, near waterfront; ample car parking
Meals breakfast
Prices rooms $-$$ with breakfast
Rooms 4 double; all have bath or shower, air-conditioning, radio, hairdrier; phone, TV by request
Facilities dining-room, 2 sitting-rooms, porch; garden, swimming-pool, spa pool
Smoking outdoors only
Credit cards MC, V
Children over 13
Disabled not suitable
Closed never
Languages English only
Proprietors Suzanne and Michael Pescitelli

Southeast

Luxury bed-and-breakfast, West Palm Beach

Hibiscus House

The glamour of this house in the revitalized Old Northwood Historic District surprises anyone who assumes that all Florida inns are informal beach-side places. The valuable Chinese vases, swagged floral drapery and boldly coloured walls are as stylish as any bed-and-breakfast in Virginia or New England. Only the views of succulent tropical foliage around the swimming-pool in the oasis-like back garden confirm that this is Florida.

The owners rescued the dilapidated 1920s home of a local mayor and transformed it into an interior decorator's dream. Although the flamboyance may be too much for some, particularly those who cannot relax in a house filled with valuable antiques, we recommend this for both price and quality.

All bedrooms have balconies or terraces, often canopied by boughs of orange trees. The Peach Room, with its collection of peach glass, has a substantial wood-canopied bed, while the Burgundy Room boasts its own private staircase. Bathrooms are not after-thoughts, but enlivened with flowers, prints and mirrors. The two-course breakfast is presented on fine china, with silverware and Waterford crystal glasses.

Nearby Palm Beach shopping, golf, polo, croquet.

501 30th Street, West Palm Beach, FL 33407
Tel and Fax (407) 863 5633; (800) 203 4927
Location corner of 30th St and Spruce St; public car parking on street
Meals breakfast
Prices rooms \$-\$\$\$ with breakfast
Rooms 5 double; 3 suites; all have bath or shower, air-conditioning, phone, TV, radio
Facilities dining-room, 2 sitting-rooms; garden, heated swimming-pool
Smoking outdoors only
Credit cards AE, MC, V
Children not suitable
Disabled not suitable
Closed never
Languages English only
Proprietors Colin Rayner and Raleigh Hill

More on page 159

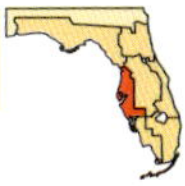

Central West

Gulfside inn, Bradenton, at Holmes Beach

Harrington House

Dark glasses are a necessity here, not just to cut the glare from the sun but also from the blinding-white, sugar-soft sand that stretches up and down the seashore as far as the eye can see. Beaches such as this are typical of the barrier islands on the Gulf Coast of Florida. Some have been ruined by development, a few remain unspoiled. Holmes Beach on Anna Maria Island is in between. There are houses and low-rise buildings but it has retained an old-fashioned, rather uncommercial feel.

Surrounded by trees and bushes, the Harrington House is right on the water, so the sound of crashing waves lulls guests to sleep at night. Built as a holiday home in 1925, the tiers of decks are designed for sunbathing and for watching the spectacular sunsets. Yet inside, we could have been in a New England inn.

The two-storey high sitting-room has a fireplace, sofas to stretch out on, and shelves of books; bedrooms have antiques and patchwork quilts. Staying here is like visiting friends: guests can borrow a sun hat, use a kayak, or take a bicycle to explore the island. Breakfasts, however, are more adventurous and satisfying than in most private homes.

Nearby beach, water sports, Sarasota.

5626 Gulf Drive, Holmes Beach, FL 34217
Tel (941) 778 5444
Fax (941) 778 0527
Location between 56 St and 58 St; ample car parking
Meals breakfast
Prices rooms $$-$$$$ with breakfast
Rooms 12 double; 1 cottage; all have bath or shower, air-conditioning, phone, TV, radio, minibar
Facilities 2 dining-rooms, sitting-room; terrace, gazebo, swimming-pool
Smoking outdoors only
Credit cards MC, V
Children over 12
Disabled access to 1 room
Closed never
Languages English only
Proprietors Jo and Frank Davis

Central West

English hotel, Inverness

The Crown Hotel

"No more hotels, we're here on vacation," Nigel and Jill Sumner told friends on their first visit to the USA in 1990. The holiday was a break after selling their hotel business in Wales. Since innkeeping is in their blood, the temptation to buy The Crown proved irresistible, perhaps because it reminded them of coaching inns found in English market towns. They carefully upgraded the furnishings, so that each of the 34 bedrooms is different. Even the smallest has carved oak trim, Victorian-style fabrics and gold-plated taps in the bathroom, where the shower is of American, not British, power. Portraits of monarchs such as Henry VIII and Queen Victoria line the stairs.

The Crown bears no relation, however, to the garish themed hotels elsewhere in Florida. The Sumners have proved that a tasteful, professionally-run, small hotel and restaurant can succeed in the land of motels and condominiums. As in Europe, it is the focal point of the community, with locals as well as visitors playing darts in the Fox and Hounds Pub, where cheeseburgers and crabcakes are as popular as fish and chips. Next door, Churchill's restaurant is for more formal dining.

Nearby Homosassa Springs Wildlife Park, boating, fishing.

109 North Seminole Avenue, Inverness, FL 34450
Tel (352) 344 5555
Fax (352) 726 4040
Location on main square; ample car parking
Meals breakfast, lunch, dinner, snacks
Prices rooms $-$$ breakfast
Rooms 34 double; all have bath or shower, air-conditioning, phone, TV
Facilities dining-room, pub, lift/elevator; terrace, swimming-pool
Smoking permitted
Credit cards AE, DC, MC, V
Children welcome
Disabled not suitable
Closed never
Languages English only
Proprietors Nigel and Jill Sumner

Central West

Bayside bed-and-breakfast, St Petersburg

Bayboro House

"I've lived here since 1982 but I'm not bored yet by the view," Gordon Powers told us. Straight across the street is the broad expanse of Tampa Bay, with its passing parade of sailboats, fishing boats, and cruise ships. This is not downtown St Petersburg, however, but an historic residential area at the southern end of the city's sprawl. Since it is only a short drive to the Gulf beaches or to the downtown area, the inn attracts couples taking a break as well as those travelling on business.

Gordon and his wife, Antonia, are highly-experienced innkeepers, whose welcome is low-key rather than overwhelming. He is the personification of dry humour; she could be a housewife from the 1950s in her white apron. They are both fans of the old, so the house looks much as it did in the early 1900s. The suitably decorous drawing-room has button-back chairs, lace curtains and etched glass, though tunes such as *Hello Dolly* on the player piano add a touch of jolly modernity. In bedrooms, patchwork or crocheted spreads top antique beds. The Powers are always making improvements. In 1996, it was extra car parking space; next, they promise a swimming-pool.

Nearby beaches, Salvador Dali museum, Bayfront Center.

1719 Beach Drive SE, St Petersburg, FL 33701
Tel and Fax (813) 823 4955
Location not far from exit 9, I-275; ample car parking
Meals breakfast, afternoon snack
Prices rooms $$ with breakfast
Rooms 3 double; 1 suite; all have bath or shower, air-conditioning, TV, VCR
Facilities dining-room, 2 sitting-rooms; veranda, garden, swimming-pool
Smoking outdoors only
Credit cards MC, V
Children not suitable
Disabled not suitable
Closed never
Languages English only
Proprietors Gordon and Antonia Powers

Central West

Historic bed-and-breakfast, St Petersburg

Mansion House

Known for years as a city of retired folk, the median age in St Petersburg is now 38. Sporty types come here to go fishing and boating on Tampa Bay and the Intracoastal Waterway, which border the metropolis. Major league baseball teams train here in the spring. Many visitors, however, come for the culture, particularly to see the Salvador Dali Museum. The Mansion House, owned by Alan and Suzanne Lucas, makes a convenient base for all these attractions since it is right in the heart of the city. This is a mixed area, where conservationists fight to save the old buildings that have escaped redevelopment.

"We are either brave our mad," Alan and Suzanne told us, admitting that gentrification is a slow process. They moved here from Wales in 1991 and soon received awards for restoring the 1904-built house which, despite the name, is not a grand place. It feels like an outpost of Wales, with homey comforts in simply-decorated bedrooms named Raglan, Caerphilly and Harlech, and individual tables in the breakfast-room where Welsh cakes are served, as well as muffins and bagels. Imagine the best of Welsh bed-breakfasts, but add sunshine. That is the Mansion House.

Nearby pier and marina, Salvador Dali Museum, Thunderdome.

105 5th Avenue NE, St Petersburg, FL 33701
Tel and Fax (813) 821 9391
Location corner of 5th Ave NE and 1st St; public car parking
Meals breakfast
Prices rooms $-$$ with breakfast
Rooms 6 double; all have bath or shower, air-conditioning, TV
Facilities dining-room, 2 sitting-rooms
Smoking outdoors only
Credit cards AE, MC, V
Children over 12
Disabled not suitable
Closed never
Languages English only
Proprietors Alan and Suzanne Lucas

Central West

Cottage complex, St Petersburg Beach

Island's End

'If you were any closer to the water, you'd have to put a swim suit on', was our inspector's reaction to this small cluster of buildings at the southern tip of St Petersburg Beach island. This is where the waters of the Intracoastal Waterway and Tampa Bay merge with the Gulf of Mexico, so constant entertainment is provided by boats of all kinds, shapes and sizes ploughing their way through the channels just offshore.

Guests fish from the dock and watch the resident pelicans dive, torpedo-like, on to their prey. Sea grape and feathery pines shade the natural wood walkways linking the small cluster of cedar cottages that are designed for casual life, so are pleasant rather than plush. Frustratingly, the swimming-pool is just for those staying in the three-bedroom house, but anyone can swim from the long, clean, sandy public beach that is only a few steps away.

This is not a traditional bed-and-breakfast: since coffee and pastries are served only three mornings a week. That is no real drawback, since all suites have kitchens and there are cafés nearby in the historic district of Pass-A-Grille Beach. Old-fashioned and quiet, this is the more attractive part of the island.

Nearby beach, boating, fishing, museums, restaurants, shopping.

1 Pass-A-Grille Way, St Petersburg Beach, FL 33706
Tel (813) 360 5023
Fax (813) 367 7890
Location on the water, at the end of the island; ample car parking
Meals breakfast on Tues, Thurs, Sat
Prices rooms $-$$$
Rooms 6 cottages; all have bath or shower, air-conditioning, phone, TV, kitchen; some whirlpool tubs; 1 with swimming-pool
Facilities decks, garden, sunbathing beach
Smoking permitted
Credit cards MC, V
Children very welcome
Disabled not suitable
Closed never
Languages Latvian, Lithuanian, Russian
Proprietors Jone and Millard Gamble

Central West

Bed-and-breakfast, Sarasota

Villa at Raintree Gardens

Sarasota has long been a tourist destination. Although the first golf course in the state was laid out here in 1886, it was millionaire circus-owner John Ringling, who put the town on the cultural map. His Venetian mansion, collection of Old Master paintings and 18thC theatre are now major attractions. Amateur botanists, however, head for the world-famous Marie Selby Gardens, known for its epiphytes, particularly orchids.

Orchids also thrive in Elizabeth Stanford's stunning screened patio. Nowhere else have we seen anything like this two-storey high, outdoor room, where the splash pool, set among black lava boulders, looks like a South Seas grotto. Beyond is her 'edible landscaping' of papaya, mango, fig and orange trees.

Elizabeth herself is a rather bohemian type, who bought this 1925-built villa on impulse. Having done it up, she furnished the rather small rooms in a style she calls 'early attic'. There are stacks of art books plus an array of antiques and collectibles, each of which has a story. Fans of uncluttered, spacious interiors might feel cramped here, but there is a nature reserve at the end of the garden and Little Sarasota Bay is just a short walk away.

Nearby Siesta Key beaches, golf, Sarasota.

1758 Vamo Drive, Sarasota, FL 34231
Tel (941) 966 6596
Fax (941) 966 6977
Location in residential area, not far from rte 41; ample car parking
Meals breakfast
Prices rooms $$ with breakfast
Rooms 2 suites; all have bath or shower, air-conditioning
Facilities dining-room, sitting-room; terrace, garden, swimming-pool
Smoking outdoors only
Credit cards not accepted
Children not suitable
Disabled not suitable
Closed Aug to mid-Sept
Languages French
Proprietor Elizabeth Stanford

Central West

Waterside complex, Sarasota, at Siesta Key

Banana Bay Club

We are happy to recommend the Banana Bay Club, even though it does not fit into any of the usual categories in this book. It is not a bed-and-breakfast, a guest-house or an hotel, but this complex of self-catering suites is small and definitely charming.

It is in a totally uncommercial area of Siesta Key island, surrounded by private homes and facing Heron Lagoon, a bird sanctuary. Osprey and green herons are regular visitors; there is even the occasional eagle.

The owner, Hannah Spencer, is always on hand. Out-going and amusing, she cheerfully admits to having dramatic decorating tastes. "The painters couldn't believe I wanted walls of deep raspberry and sea-green." She does nothing by halves, and pushed the safari theme in number 7 through to the limit, with leopard print cushions, zebra-striped bedspreads and an animal shower-curtain. It all adds up to a fun, comfortable and convenient place to stay. There is a small swimming-pool but only a few minutes away are the long white sands along the Gulf and also Turtle Beach, popular with shell-hunters. Shops and restaurants are nearby; Sarasota is just across the causeway.

Nearby beaches, shopping, tennis, golf, Sarasota museums.

8524 Midnight Pass Road,
Sarasota, FL 34242
Tel (941) 346 0113
Fax (941) 349 4161
Location at southern end of Siesta Key, off Sarasota; ample car parking
Meals no meals served
Prices rooms $$-$$$$
Suites 7; all have bath or shower, air-conditioning, phone, TV, kitchen
Facilities swimming-pool, deck, dock, boats, bicycles
Smoking permitted
Credit cards not accepted
Children very welcome
Disabled access to 1 room
Closed never
Languages English only
Proprietors Hannah and Bob Spencer

Central West

Hacienda-style house, Venice

The Banyan House

Venice started life as a fishing village, but was transformed into a retirement community in the 1920s. Early 'snowbirds' included the Brotherhood of Locomotive Engineers; 30 years later, the circus came to town, when the Ringling Brothers Barnum & Bailey troupes made it their winter headquarters. Their rehearsals are open to the public. Otherwise, the town is quiet and sedate, with some of the best beaches on the Gulf, where fossilised shark's teeth sometimes are washed ashore.

The Banyan House is part of the history of Venice. Built in 1926, it is not only one of the oldest homes, but also claims to have the first swimming-pool. Locals Chuck and Susan McCormick restored the Spanish-Mediterranean style hacienda, with its watch-tower and barrel-tiled roof, its coffered ceiling and wrought iron banister. Although the furniture and paintings are not as grand as the architecture, this is a quiet and comfortable place for couples and older folk to stay.

Open since 1987, the McCormicks remain admirably enthusiastic despite being the longest-established bed-and-breakfast in the area.

Nearby circus winter headquarters, beaches, golf.

519 South Harbor Drive,
Venice, FL 34285
Tel (941) 484 1385
Location in residential area; ample car parking
Meals breakfast
Prices rooms $$ with breakfast
Rooms 9 double; all have bath or shower, air-conditioning, TV, radio, minibar; some phone
Facilities sitting-room; patio, decks, garden, swimming-pool
Smoking outdoors only
Credit cards not accepted
Children over 12
Disabled not suitable
Closed 2 weeks August
Languages English only
Proprietors Chuck and Susan McCormick

More on page 160

Central

Historic bed-and-breakfast, Bartow

Stanford Inn

Even Americans who know Florida well haven't heard of Bartow, yet they may have seen the Stanford Inn in the film *My Girl*, where it was the funeral home. There is nothing depressing, however, about this mansion. Built in 1900, it was owned by descendants of the original family until 1983 when antiques-dealer Freddie Guess came to look at furniture and 'ended up buying the house'. After a total renovation, he moved in his outstanding collection of fine art and furniture and opened to guests in 1995. The Napoleon III suite is named for the focal point, the French Emperor's own desk; the Old Master Suite has portraits of King Charles I and Queen Henrietta Maria by Van Dyck. Yet bathrooms are luxuriously modern and rooms all have ironing boards and irons because many guests are on business.

Although professional in attitude, Freddie has a strong sense of humour, cheerfully admitting that the deep colour of the Purple Suite is overwhelming. Lighter and brighter are the Hibiscus Suite and the Old Caretaker's Cottage in the garden, where high hedges guard the swimming-pool. "Like staying in a museum," was one reaction. "You don't expect to find this in Florida."

Nearby Bok Tower, Cypress Gardens; antiques shopping.

555 East Stanford Street, Bartow, FL 33830
Tel/Fax (941) 533 2393
Location in Historic District; car parking on quiet street
Meals breakfast
Prices rooms \$-\$\$\$ with breakfast
Rooms 2 double; 4 suites; 2 cottages; all have bath or shower, air-conditioning, phone, TV, radio, hairdrier, iron and ironing board
Facilities dining-room, 4 sitting-rooms; veranda, terrace, garden, heated swimming-pool
Smoking restricted
Credit cards AE, MC, V
Children over 10
Disabled not suitable
Closed never
Languages English only
Proprietor Freddie Guess

Central

Victorian bed-and-breakfast, Eustis

Dreamspinner

Eustis makes a useful base for exploring the lake region or antiques-hunting in the New England-like town of Mt Dora, only 5 miles (8 km) to the south. Even the city of Orlando is only 30 miles (48 km) away. Eustis itself, however, is an unassuming place, so the hint of sophistication in this 1881-built house comes as a surprise. A faint foreign accent in the hushed voice of the owner, Jeano Broom, reflects the years she lived in Europe. Here, she has created a neat and tidy clapboard home whose broad porch overlooks old trees, well-tended flowers and a garden large enough for a game of croquet.

Inside are fresh flowers, English fabrics and modest, rather than priceless, antiques from both the Old and New Worlds. A handsome black onyx fireplace is the focal point of the parlour; upstairs, a picket fence serves as an unusual headboard in the Potting Room. The old-fashioned bathrooms have the usual claw-foot tubs. A traditionalist in the best sense, Jeano hangs washed sheets to dry outdoors to give them a fresh scent and chats over an English-style tea or wine and cheese. Be sure to get precise directions: route signs can be confusing in this area.

Nearby Mt Dora, lakes.

117 Diedrich Street, Eustis, FL 32726
Tel (352) 589 8082
Location in small town; ample car parking
Meals breakfast, afternoon snacks
Prices rooms $-$$ with breakfast
Rooms 4 double; all have bath or shower, air-conditioning
Facilities dining-room, sitting-room; garden, croquet, bicycles
Smoking outdoors only
Credit cards AE, MC, V
Children over 12
Disabled not suitable
Closed never
Languages English only
Proprietor Jeano Broom

Central

Country inn, Lake Wales

Chalet Suzanne

'The Chalet' as locals call it, is a Florida institution, family-run and much favoured for weddings and anniversaries. The restaurant's soup became famous when Apollo 15 astronauts took some, freeze-dried, to the moon. Now, the on-site cannery produces soups for the gift shop. This booming business started in 1931 when widow Bertha Hinshaw offered meals and rooms to the public to support her two children. Success enabled her to travel and souvenirs from Europe and the Middle East create a curiously eclectic look. Antique Persian and English tiles are set in walls and on tables, the bar is 'Norwegian', while an Italian altar angel simpers in one of the five dining-rooms. There, waitresses in pseudo-dirndls serve six-course dinners that are traditional rather than trendy, featuring baked chicken Suzanne or filet mignon.

Bedroom decoration ranges from 'rustic' to 'plush chintz'; some bathrooms have box-like baths lined in colourful tiles, others boast new walk-in showers.

At night, when tiny lights outline the buildings, the complex looks like an outpost of Disney's Magic Kingdom. Reactions vary: some enthuse, others think the experience is over-priced.
Nearby Bok Tower Gardens, Cypress Gardens.

3800 Chalet Suzanne Drive, Lake Wales, FL 33853
Tel (941) 676 6011; (800) 433 6011
Fax (941) 676 1814
Location on country road off route 27; ample car parking
Meals breakfast, lunch, dinner
Prices rooms $$$-$$$$ with breakfast
Rooms 30 double; all have bath or shower, air-conditioning, phone, TV
Facilities 5 dining-rooms, 2 sitting-rooms, bar; terrace, garden, swimming-pool, badminton, private airstrip
Smoking permitted
Credit cards AE, DC, MC, V
Children very welcome
Disabled 1 room adapted
Closed never; restaurant only, Monday
Languages German
Proprietors Carl and Vita Hinshaw

Central

Lakeside bed-and-breakfast, Maitland

Thurston House

Thurston House offers a welcome refuge from Greater Orlando, whose daunting traffic and maelstrom of highways and expressways are only 5 miles (8 km) away. A long driveway leads to wooded park-like grounds, with flowers, fruit trees and lawns running down to Lake Eulalia, one of 14 lakes in Maitland.

The gabled roof and wrap-around porch are typical of vacation homes built a century ago for wealthy northern families. The present owner, Carole Ballard, began renovating the building from the basement upwards in 1992 and the result is more of a micro-hotel than a bed-and-breakfast. While not all furniture is antique, it is well-chosen and set off by gleaming hardwood floors.

Each bedroom is different, but all have a desk and a telephone, which appeals to those travelling on business. Hirsch boasts a canopy over the bed, as well as an old-fashioned sleeping porch with a double hammock. O'Heir, with a handsome pine mantle over the fireplace, overlooks the lake. All bathrooms are modern and efficient with space to lay out toiletries. Carole is welcoming and attentive without being intrusive; she seems born to be an innkeeper.

Nearby Orlando and amusement parks.

851 Lake Avenue, Maitland, FL 32751
Tel (407) 539 1911; (800) 843 2721
Location in residential area; ample car parking
Meals breakfast
Prices rooms $$ with breakfast
Rooms 4 double; all have bath or shower, air-conditioning, phone, radio
Facilities dining-room, 2 sitting-rooms; porch, garden
Smoking outdoors only
Credit cards AE, MC, V
Children over 12
Disabled not suitable
Closed never
Languages English only
Proprietor Carole Ballard

Central

Bed-and-breakfast, Mount Dora

Amapola 'Villa of the Poppies'

The ballad *Amapola* was a hit 70 years ago and has been recorded regularly ever since. Its composer was the grandfather of innkeeper Dolores Bersell, who admits that the song's royalties "paid for the house" which she and her husband, Bob, bought in 1993. Forget the Victorian look of many bed-and-breakfasts; here, the Bersells have recreated the art deco era. From the handsome walnut dining-room furniture to a Tiffany stained glass lampshade in the sunroom, the decoration shows a flair that continues in the three distinctive bedrooms. Isadora's has furniture crafted of amboina, a rare Malaysian wood, plus an unusual 17-piece dresser set. Every object seems to tell a story, from the Bersells' collections of Van Briggle pottery and Lladró figures to the mementoes of the song *Amapola* and its creator. Despite the subtitle, Villa of the Poppies, gardenias and camellias also thrive in the lush gardens and there is even an orchid house.

Mt Dora grew up by one of 14,000 lakes in a region which also has rolling hills, pasture and hardwood trees. Well known for antiques shops and photogenic old houses, the town can be crowded during the many festivals held throughout the year.

Nearby water sports, golf; 25 miles (40 km) from Orlando.

347 East Third Avenue, Mount Dora, FL 32757
Tel (352) 735 3800; (800) 776 2112
Location heart of town; ample car parking
Meals breakfast
Prices rooms $$-$$$ with breakfast
Rooms 2 double; 1 suite; all have bath or shower, air-conditioning
Facilities 2 dining-rooms, 2 sitting-rooms; garden, hot tub
Smoking not permitted
Credit cards AE, MC, V
Children not suitable
Disabled not suitable
Closed never
Languages English only
Proprietors Bob and Dolores Bersell

Central

Bed-and-breakfast, Mount Dora

Darst Victorian Manor

Jim and Nanci Darst came from Oklahoma, looking for the perfect old house to turn into a bed-and-breakfast. When they could not find their ideal, they built it. The result is a pleasing grey and blue reproduction of a Queen Anne mansion from the 1880s, complete with miles of white trim. Not a detail is overlooked or understated. Bold colours are fearlessly combined with even bolder floral patterns; the result can be overwhelming, though the comforts are undeniable. The Priscilla Room is black and pink, Oak Splendor is green, blue, pink and gold.

Our favourite, Queen Victoria, is a three-room suite with its own turret and views over Lake Dora. It is right at the top of this three-storey house, so is not recommended for those who have difficulty with stairs. The Priscilla, however, on the ground floor, is adapted for wheelchair-users. For some, the absence of bedroom telephones and televisions is a boon; for others, a drawback. Nanci is a gregarious hostess and an enthusiastic breakfast chef, with plenty of secret recipes for dishes such as cream cheese-filled French bread toast. Opened in 1995, this inn has become popular with weekend antiques hunters.

Nearby water sports, golf; 25 miles (40 km) from Orlando.

495 Old Highway 441, Mt Dora, FL 32757
Tel (352) 383 4050
Location 2 blocks west of downtown; ample car parking
Meals breakfast
Prices rooms $$$-$$$$ with breakfast
Rooms 4 double; 1 suite; all have bath or shower, air-conditioning
Facilities dining-room, 2 sitting-rooms; veranda, garden
Smoking not permitted, strictly enforced
Credit cards AE, MC, V
Children over 12
Disabled 1 adapted room
Closed never
Languages English only
Proprietors Jim and Nanci Darst

Central

Country bed-and-breakfast, Ocala

Heritage Country Inn

Horses are big business here, with some 400 stud farms raising breeds ranging from Clydesdales to miniatures. The renown of the county, however, is built on thoroughbreds, including five winners of the prestigious Kentucky Derby. Right in the middle of the lush, rolling hills stands this single-storey, lemon-yellow complex which opened in 1994.

Carpentry was always a hobby for Harold Coutts, so when he and his wife 'retired' to Florida, he built this bed-and-breakfast, making all the handsome furniture himself. Each of the six spacious bedrooms has its own entrance and individual decoration. The Homestead room looks rustic, with cypress panelling offset by local stone; Audubon is in restful blue and white; while Thoroughbred is 'country English' with walls of polished oak. Bathrooms are equally well-designed. The four-poster beds, wood-burning fireplaces, comfortable furnishings and bargain prices have tempted some guests to settle in for weeks.

We were particularly impressed by the careful adaptation of the rooms for wheelchairs. Even the built-in cupboards are fitted with an additional, lower rail.

Nearby stud farms, riding, golf, Ocala National Forest.

14343 West Highway 40,
Ocala, FL 34481
Tel (352) 489 0023
Location 11.5 miles (17.5 km) west of I-75 via exit 69; ample car parking
Meals breakfast
Prices rooms $ with breakfast
Rooms 6 double, all have bath or shower, air-conditioning, phone, TV
Facilities dining-room, sitting-room; garden, swimming-pool
Smoking outdoors only
Credit cards DC, MC, V
Children over 12
Disabled 6 rooms adapted
Closed never
Languages English only
Proprietors Harold and Leo Coutts

Central

Art deco hotel, Ocala

The Ritz

Some 60 years ago, locals dubbed Ocala 'the Hollywood of the East' when films such as *Tarzan* were made nearby in Silver Springs. Then, the road outside The Ritz was dirt, not tarmac. Now route 40 is a main thoroughfare and, although a high wall blots out the sight of traffic, its noise is still noticeable at the swimming-pool. That, however, is the only drawback to staying in this hotel where a total overhaul in 1987 converted the original 16 apartments to 32 suites. In a 'standard', the bedroom is separate from the sitting-room, while the larger 'executive' suites are open-plan, with fireplaces plus private screened porches or balconies. In these, cane furniture, venetian blinds and hardwood floors create an uncluttered look, while bathrooms have large mirrors with first-class lighting. The art deco theme is strongest in the central sitting area, where a pianist plays in the evenings and a breakfast buffet is set out in the morning.

Across the garden, shaded by live oaks, stands the Pavilion, which caters for small functions. Already popular with business travellers, the microwaves, small fridges and coffee makers, let alone the attractive prices, would suit holidaymakers as well.
Nearby golf, riding, Silver Springs, Ocala National Forest.

1205 East Silver Springs Boulevard, Ocala, FL 34470
Tel (352) 867 7700
Fax (352) 867 9618
Location on route 40, east of downtown Ocala; ample car parking
Meals breakfast
Prices rooms $-$$ with breakfast
Rooms 32 suites; all have bath or shower, air-conditioning, phone, TV, fridge, hairdrier; microwave oven, coffee-maker
Facilities dining-room, sitting-room/bar, terrace, garden, swimming-pool
Smoking outdoors only
Credit cards AE, MC, V
Children very welcome
Disabled 2 rooms adapted
Closed never
Languages Spanish
Manager Gary Merritt

Central

Historic bed-and-breakfast, Ocala

Seven Sisters Inn

"I'd never heard of Ocala before we came here." That was in 1990; now Bonnie Morehardt is an enthusiastic supporter of the revitalisation of the Historic District in what remains a little-known city. From the main square, Fort King Street stretches east, lined with tall trees and large houses such as this 1888-built inn.

Where some bed-and-breakfasts aim for a family atmosphere, this is a business; weddings are popular and special packages include Murder Mystery Weekends. The house is full of remembrances of things past, from old hats on a stand to a wind-up music box. Bedrooms, however, are dramatically and densely decorated. Ken's Room is Chinese red with one black and white-striped wall and a whirlpool tub in the corner. Sylvia's room is 'pulsating pink', according to one guest. Those preferring 'quieter' furnishings should ask for Lottie's Loft, the attic, reached by steep stairs. Here, a skylight in the angled roof brightens the neutral tones. Unlike most bed-and-breakfasts, dinner is offered most weekends or by special request.

Changes in 1996 include renovating the outside as well as redecorating and creating new rooms inside.

Nearby golf, riding, Ocala National Forest, Silver Springs.

820 SE Fort King Street,
Ocala, FL 34471
Tel (352) 867 1170
Fax (352) 867 5266
Location in city's Historic District; ample car parking
Meals breakfast, dinner by request, afternoon tea
Prices rooms $$-$$$ with breakfast
Rooms 7 double; 1 suite; all have bath or shower, air-conditioning, radio; some phone, TV
Facilities dining-room, sitting-room; veranda, garden
Smoking outdoors only
Credit cards AE, MC, V
Children over 12
Disabled access 1 room
Closed never
Languages Spanish, Swedish
Proprietors Bonnie Morehardt and Ken Oden

Central

Historic bed-and-breakfast, Orlando

Courtyard at Lake Lucerne

In a city better-known for its 1,000 room hotels, it is hard to believe that a charming small hotel exists. Attorney Charles Meiner bought the oldest house in Orlando, the 1883 Norment-Parry mansion, then added two neighbouring buildings to create the courtyard of the name. Lavishly planted, with brick walkways and a Dutch fountain, this is the focus for what has grown into a 22-bedroom hotel.

Each house follows a different style. The Norment-Parry has Victorian-style brass bedsteads, overstuffed chairs and patterned fabrics. Our inspector liked number 104 which, although cozy, has 'the world's smallest bathroom'.

Less cluttered and more masculine is the Edwardian I W Phillips House, with its Tiffany stained-glass window and 18thC Flemish painting. For sybarites, the Pink Honeymoon Suite boasts a steam room plus a double bath and whirlpool tub. In contrast, the Wellborn House is a temple of art deco, with vases, lamps and zebra-striped sofas.

Some may find the intensity of the themed decoration offers little respite after a day at Disney. With a busy staff, the feel here is brisk and businesslike rather than homey and personal.

Nearby Disney complex, downtown Orlando.

211 North Lucerne Circle East, Orlando, FL 32801
Tel (407) 648 5188; (800) 444 5289
Fax (407) 246 1368
Location near East-West Expressway in Orlando; ample car parking
Meals breakfast
Prices rooms $-$$$ with breakfast
Rooms 6 double; 16 suites; all have bath or shower, air-conditioning, phone, TV; some Jacuzzi, kitchenettes
Facilities dining-room, several sitting-rooms; garden
Smoking outdoors only
Credit cards AE, MC, V
Children over 12
Disabled not suitable
Closed never
Languages English only
Proprietors Meiner Family Partnership

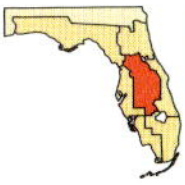

Central

Bed-and-breakfast, Orlando

The Veranda

In 1994, true to American bed-and-breakfast tradition, Blair Colby rescued an attractive building from ruin. He even drafted the code which now regulates the city's bed-and-breakfasts. The Veranda has no communal rooms, so 'everything seems to go on outside', according to our inspector. Luckily, the two verandas are lined with white rocking chairs and there is also a garden. Here, walkways and gates, a gazebo and a hot tub, lush foliage and a swimming-pool all crowd into the small lot in the revived historic district of downtown Orlando. Colby and his partners have gone on to purchase a neighbouring property which should provide some much needed additional space.

The style is vigorously Key West and tropical; this is not the sort of inn where guests gather round the cosy parlour fireplace. It is popular with business people and also a favourite for holding weddings, so be sure no functions are planned if you are hoping for a quiet break. Bedrooms are small yet stylish enough and named Europa, Victorian, or Erté, in tribute to the French designer. All have small but modern bathrooms. Breakfast may be taken in your bedroom or in the courtyard.

Nearby 25 min drive from Disney.

115 North Summerlin Avenue, Orlando, FL 32801
Tel (407) 849 0321; (800) 420 6822
Location at N Summerlin and Jefferson; public car parking on street
Meals breakfast
Prices rooms $$-$$$$ with breakfast
Rooms 4 double; 2 suites; all have bath or shower, air-conditioning, phone, TV
Facilities porches, garden, swimming-pool, hot tub
Smoking not permitted
Credit cards AE, MC, V
Children over 12
Disabled 1 adapted room
Closed never
Languages English only
Proprietor Blair Colby

Central

Bed-and-breakfast, Orlando at Lake Buena Vista

PerriHouse

The area southwest of Orlando is a land of theme parks and huge hotels, yet right on the doorstep of Walt Disney World is the Perri House. Built, owned and run by the Perretti family since 1990, its six bedrooms make it a minnow amongst whales. Nick is a New Yorker of Italian background, Angie hails from Miami and their daughters help out at weekends. The folksy flavour is established in the 'history hallway', with its montage of Perretti photos and maps stuck with pins marking guests' home towns.

"People don't come here to relax," Nick admits, "they want to do it all." So, bedrooms are practical, with outside entrances and comfortable rather than designer furnishings. Number 2 has dark cherry reproduction furniture; number 6 has a white oak four-poster bed and bright, sunflower-print curtains. Professionally-run, with keen prices, this is one of the most family-friendly places we have inspected, with highchairs, cribs and use of laundry facilities. Those tired of sightseeing use the swimming-pool or bird-watch in the extensive grounds which are now a nature reserve. Over the years, guests have contributed to the extraordinary collection of 300 bird-houses.

Nearby Disney World, Universal Studios, Sea World.

PO Box 22005, 10417 State Road 535, Lake Buena Vista, FL 32830
Tel (407) 876 4830; (800) 780 4830
Fax (407) 876 0241
Location near to Walt Disney World Resort, phone for directions; ample car parking
Meals breakfast
Prices rooms $-$$ with breakfast
Rooms 5 double; 1 family; all have bath or shower, air-conditioning, phone
Facilities dining-room, sitting-room; terrace, garden, swimming-pool, hot tub
Smoking outdoors only
Credit cards AE, MC, V
Children very welcome
Disabled not suitable
Closed never
Languages English only
Proprietors Nick and Angi Perretti

Central

Country bed-and-breakfast, Winter Haven

JD's Southern Oaks

For years, Juanita and Dallas Abercrombie drove past a dilapidated 70-year old house and dreamed of buying it. In 1989 they did and moved the entire building to their land outside Winter Haven. After two years of remodelling, the result is a spacious home with handsome antiques and no excessive Victorian frills. The Rose Garden room's colours are a restful burgundy and grey; its bathroom is prettily old-fashioned but with modern shower power. Blue Pond and the Country Penthouse are similar in feel but out in the carriage house, two suites, Sunflower and Americana, have a more rustic look.

Dallas is a handyman and justifiably proud of his latest creation, the Hayloft in the barn, where split-wood panels make the large upstairs room look like a log cabin. We particularly liked the witty WC, like a bucolic outhouse but with modern plumbing hidden beneath the two-hole seat. The Abercrombies are the kind of innkeepers who, without affectation, make guests feel like old friends. With roosters crowing in the morning and cows grazing in the fields, the feel is rural, yet Cypress Gardens are only a 10-min drive away and even Disney World is only 30 min.

Nearby Cypress Gardens, Bok Tower, Lakeland antiques shops.

3800 Country Club Road,
Winter Haven, FL 33881
Tel (941) 293 2335; (800) 771 6257
Fax (941) 299 4141
Location on farm near Lake Region Country Club; ample car parking
Meals breakfast
Prices rooms $$-$$$ with breakfast
Rooms 4 double; 2 suites; all have bath or shower, air-conditioning, phone, radio, hairdrier; 1 kitchen
Facilities dining-room, sitting-room; porch, garden
Smoking outdoors only
Credit cards not accepted
Children over 10
Disabled not suitable
Closed never
Languages English only
Proprietors Juanita and Dallas Abercrombie

Central

Bed-and-breakfast, Winter Park

The Fortnightly Inn

After the overgrown sprawl of nearby Orlando, Winter Park comes as a welcome surprise. The atmosphere is affluent, with impressive homes, up-scale shops, two museums and Rollins College. The rather plain-looking inn faces a busy street in the middle of town. Inside, the large living-room with its piano doubles as a what the hosts call a 'reception parlour'. Although the chairs and sofa look comfortable, they would not tempt us to slip off our shoes and settle back into the cushions. In the dining-room, china and silver are displayed on the large table. We found the mood formal, refined and slightly impersonal.

Bedrooms are varied, but all have large windows and plenty of light by which to appreciate the handsome furniture. Number 1 has a mahogany sleigh bed plus Empire furniture on the porch.On the ground floor, number 5 has a huge iron bed as well as an oak dresser and matching armoire. Bathrooms are on the small side.

With its rather sedate ambience, younger or more casual visitors may feel they have to be on their best behaviour. The house rules request quiet after 10 pm; breakfast is between 8 am and 9 am unless by prior arrangement.

Nearby shopping; Orlando; amusement parks, golf.

377 East Fairbanks Ave,
Winter Park, FL 32789
Tel (407) 645 4440
Location in heart of town; limited car parking
Meals breakfast
Prices rooms $$ with breakfast
Rooms 3 double; 2 suites; all have bath or shower, air-conditioning
Facilities dining-room, 2 sitting-rooms; bicycles
Smoking outdoors only
Credit cards MC, V
Children over 12
Disabled not suitable
Closed never
Languages English only
Proprietors Frank and Judi Daley

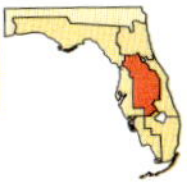

Central

Town hotel, Winter Park

Park Plaza Hotel

The name sets the tone, evoking memories of European 'park hotels' and the atmosphere inside continues the theme. The entrance is hushed and a little dark, with wood-panelling and gilt-framed pictures. Any thoughts that the staff might be stuffy, pretentious or snobby, however, were immediately dispelled by the friendly and helpful young concierge, whose guidance would be useful for first-time visitors to the Orlando area.

Built as a hotel in 1920, the Park Plaza is surrounded by shops and restaurants and faces City Park, with its benches, roses and old oak trees. Bedrooms are comfortable and pleasing rather than designer-decorated; 11 have balconies with seating and flowers. Number 224, for example, has an exposed brick wall, a brass bed, ceiling fans, potted ferns and a view of the park. Bathrooms are adequate rather than luxurious. Under separate management but integrated into the hotel is the conservatory-like Park Plaza Gardens restaurant with its brick floor, glass ceiling and plenty of greenery. Sunday brunch here is a local institution. We recommend this as an elegant alternative to the camaraderie of many bed-and-breakfasts.

Nearby shopping; Orlando, amusement parks.

307 Park Avenue South, Winter Park, FL 32789
Tel (407) 647 1072; (800) 228 7220
Fax (407) 647 4081
Location in downtown area; ample car parking
Meals breakfast, lunch, dinner
Prices rooms $$-$$$$ with breakfast
Rooms 27 double; all have bath or shower, air-conditioning, phone, TV
Facilities restaurant, sitting-room, bar, lift/elevator
Smoking restricted
Credit cards AE, DC, MC, V
Children over 5
Disabled not suitable
Closed never
Languages Spanish
Proprietors Spang family

More on page 166

Central East

Ocean-side hotel, Cocoa Beach

The Inn at Cocoa Beach

Want to watch the launches at Kennedy Space Center from your balcony? No other hotel in this guide offers such entertainment. On ordinary days, the view is 'just' of the Atlantic Ocean across a long expanse of soft-sand beach. 'It may have 50 rooms but you would never know it,' insisted our inspector, who was put off initially by the bland, modern roadside exterior. Once inside, however, he changed his mind. Although business-like, the white and mauve reception area is comfortable, with sofas and chairs for sitting and perusing local restaurant menus. In the breakfast-room, country-style pine furniture looks just like an Austrian or German small hotel. The honeymoon suites have Jacuzzis in the bedrooms; otherwise, rooms are much the same but furnished with care, from oriental porcelains and brass lamps to fresh flowers and tempting books. Bathrooms have plenty of counter space, endless hot water and first-rate towels. 'No having to search under claw foot tubs to retrieve your toiletries.' Tango, a parrot, Cocoa, a dog, and Mr Tibbs, a cat are the house pets.

Overall, the hotel combines the personal touch of a small inn with the comforts of a four-star hotel.

Nearby Kennedy Space Center, wildlife refuge.

4300 Ocean Beach Boulevard, Cocoa Beach, FL 32931
Tel (407) 799 3460: (800) 343 5307
Fax (407) 784 8632
Location on the beach at SR-520 behind Ron-Jon's Surf Shop; ample car parking
Meals breakfast, afternoon snack
Prices rooms $$-$$$$ with breakfast
Rooms 50 double; all have bath or shower, air-conditioning, phone, TV; some Jacuzzi
Facilities dining-room, sitting-room, lift/elevator; patio, swimming-pool
Smoking permitted
Credit cards AE, MC, V
Children very welcome
Disabled access to 6 rooms
Closed never
Languages English only
Manager Amy Donaghy

Central East

Historic inn, Daytona Beach

Live Oak Inn

Daytona's reputation was built on speed. The 23-mile (37 km) long beach was hard and flat enough for land speed record attempts at the turn of the century. Cars can still drive on to parts of the beach (top speed 10 mph, 16 kmph), but nowadays racing is restricted to the famous Speedway.

The previous owners of the Live Oak Inn had a love affair with machines and themed many of their rooms to attract auto fans. After Del and Jessie Glock took over in 1995, only two of those rooms survived renovation. One honours local legend, Bill France, the starter of the Daytona 500 motor race. Another, the Harley, has photos of the famous motor cycles on the walls.

Don't be put off: the inn, a pair of 19thC houses, is a far cry from the motels and fast food of popular Daytona. Located in the residential area around Halifax Harbor Marina, it overlooks the massive oaks for which it is named, as well as boats. The newly-decorated rooms verge on the plain, but that suits guests, who are happy to be far from the madding motor-sport crowd and close to the in-house restaurant, run by Tom Papa, whose menus draw on Italian, Californian and Caribbean influences.

Nearby beach, golf, water sports.

448 South Beach Street, Daytona Beach, FL 32114
Tel (904) 252 4667; (800) 253 INNS
Fax (904) 254 1871
Location at Beach St and Loomis St; ample car parking
Meals breakfast, afternoon tea, dinner
Prices rooms $$ with breakfast
Rooms 13 double; all have bath or shower, air-conditioning, phone, TV
Facilities 2 dining-rooms, sitting-room, bar; garden, dockage
Smoking outdoors only
Credit cards AE, DC, MC, V
Children not suitable
Disabled not suitable
Closed never; restaurant only Mon
Languages English only
Proprietors Del and Jessie Glock

Central East

Historic mansion, Daytona Beach

The Villa

Every year, thousands of university students descend on Daytona Beach for their spring vacation. Add in the International Speedway and high-rise hotels along the beach and the result does not appear to promise charming small hotels. There is, however, an historic district of old buildings, one of which is The Villa. Extensive lawns provide privacy for the mansion, a classic example of Florida's 'Spanish' architecture of the 1920s.

Forget the antiques of most upmarket bed-and-breakfasts. The inn is almost an art gallery, with Russian icons here, Chinese jade there and busts of Spanish nobility in the baronial dining-room, with its massive, carved table and chairs. Bedrooms are spectacular, with dramatic black and gold-lacquered furniture in Marco Polo and a baroque canopy bed in King Juan Carlos. For some, the showy overstatement may be too much like a Hollywood version of a Spanish palace. It is balanced, however, by the down-to-earth naturalness of owner Jim Camp and Annabelle, his old black Labrador dog. A swimming-pool and hot tub are in the garden, while the famous beach only a short walk away is a must for an evening walk or run.

Nearby beach, water sports, International Speedway, shopping.

801 North Peninsula Drive, Daytona Beach, FL 32118
Tel and Fax (904) 248 2020
Location between Intracoastal Waterway and beach; ample car parking
Meals breakfast
Prices rooms $-$$$ with breakfast
Rooms 4 double; all have bath or shower, air-conditioning, TV
Facilities dining-room, 2 sitting-rooms; terrace, garden, swimming-pool, hot tub
Smoking outdoors only
Credit cards AE, MC, V
Children not suitable
Disabled not suitable
Closed never
Languages English only
Proprietors Jim Camp

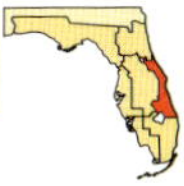

Central East

Historic house, DeLand

The 1888 House

No prizes for guessing the age of the house, which was enlarged early in the 20th century and given the pillars and portico of Classical Revival architecture. It stands in the residential part of DeLand, which is 25 miles (40 km) inland from Daytona Beach. Named for its founder, the town was designed as a Utopian community. Now its claim to fame is Stetson University, the state's oldest private university, whose campus, just a few blocks away, is very much part of the town.

A high ceiling gives an impression of stateliness to the entrance and well-chosen antiques include Mary Lindenmeyer's own collection of Hummel porcelain in the dining-room, where a communal breakfast is served at 8.30 am. Bedrooms range from the smallest, Emily's, through Jewel's, which has its own sunroom, to Coralinn's, the most spacious with a corner fireplace and bay window. The decoration is cream or white, with accents of colour and wall-to-wall carpeting that feels lush underfoot.

In short, the graciousness of the house reflects the personality of the innkeeper. Guests relax on the veranda, borrow bicycles or explore several state parks nearby.

Nearby fishing, golf, water sports, wildlife refuge, skydiving.

124 North Clara Avenue,
DeLand, FL 32720
Tel (904) 822 4647
Location in quiet residential area; ample car parking
Meals breakfast, lunch, dinner, snacks
Prices rooms $-$$ with breakfast
Rooms 3 double; all have bath or shower, air-conditioning
Facilities dining-room, sitting-room; veranda, garden
Smoking outdoors only
Credit cards MC, V
Children not suitable
Disabled not suitable
Closed never
Languages English only
Proprietor Mary Lindenmeyer

Central East

Seaside inn, Jensen Beach

Hutchinson Inn

Long and thin, Hutchinson Island stretches some 20 miles (32 km) between Stuart and Fort Pierce. At the southern end, buildings are restricted to four stories; once into St Lucie County high rise condominiums dominate the beach front. An exception is the Hutchinson Inn.

What was originally a two-storey motel-like structure was transformed in 1991 by Tony and Cathy Fillichio into a small inn that recalls 'old Florida' but has up-to-date conveniences. Concrete walls are painted pink and trimmed with white railings and blue awnings. An aviary of parakeets greets guests on their way to check in at the front desk, an old English pub bar with decorative carvings and glass panels.

The hotel is right on the beach with its own heated swimming-pool. Only a few rooms, however, face the ocean; the rest have side views. Furnishings in pale peach with teal blue are comfortable rather than plush. Most rooms have small kitchenettes and some interconnect, which is popular with families, as are the laundry facilities and Saturday cook-outs. February, however, tends to attract an older clientele without children.

Nearby tennis, watersports, golf; Stuart.

9750 South Ocean Drive (rte A1A), Jensen Beach, FL 34957
Tel (407) 229 2000
Fax (407) 229 8875
Location on Hutchinson Island beach, north of Stuart; ample car parking
Meals breakfast, Saturday barbecue
Prices rooms $-$$$$ with breakfast
Rooms 20 double; 1 suite; all have bath or shower, air-conditioning, phone, TV, radio; most have kitchenettes
Facilities terrace, heated swimming-pool, tennis court
Smoking outdoors only
Credit cards MC, V
Children very welcome
Disabled not suitable
Closed never
Languages English only
Proprietors Tony and Cathy Fillichio

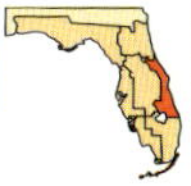

Central East

Town bed-and-breakfast, Lake Helen

Clauser's Bed & Breakfast

Just off Route 4, the Interstate highway that links tourist spots such as Orlando and Daytona Beach, is the sleepy little town of Lake Helen. Standing on a side street is this large white house, built in 1895, and retaining the look of a pleasant old farmhouse. Red rocking chairs on a blue porch and an amiable clutter of family history and belongings reflect the style of the two generations of Clausers who run the inn.

Some bed-and-breakfasts try too hard to be special; here the atmosphere is homey and straightforward. At the end of a day, guests congregate in Sherlock's, the English-style pub in the converted Carriage House. Bedrooms follow themes, but the result is 'fun' rather than contrived. Laredo has a cedar log interior and a real horse trough for a bathtub, while in Cross Creek, a porch railing serves as a headboard. Those who fancy whirlpool tubs should book into Lexington or Charlevoix. Be in the dining-room at 9 am for a sit-down country breakfast of eggs, meats and biscuits, a scone-like Southern speciality.

Murder Mystery Weekends are a trend throughout Florida bed-and-breakfasts and Clauser's is no exception.

Nearby antiques shopping; Atlantic beaches 45 min away.

201 East Kicklighter Road,
Lake Helen, FL 32744
Tel (904) 228 0310; (800) 220 0310
Fax (904) 228 2337
Location on quiet street in small town; ample car parking
Meals breakfast
Prices rooms $-$$ with breakfast
Rooms 8 double; all have bath or shower, air-conditioning, phone; some TV, Jacuzzi
Facilities dining-room, sitting-room, pub; porch, garden, gazebo with hot tub
Smoking outdoors only
Credit cards AE, DC, MC, V
Children over 16
Disabled 2 adapted rooms
Closed never
Languages English only
Proprietors Clauser and Roy families

Central East

Waterside hotel, New Smyrna Beach

Night Swan

Entertainment is free at the Night Swan. Pelicans fly past, looking for lunch; dolphins play in the water; and sailboats, yachts and canoes make their way up and down Indian River, part of the Intracoastal Waterway. Guests can watch from the private dock, the wrap-around porch and the bedrooms of the 1906-built house, whose numerous windows are angled to catch even the slightest summer breeze.

Everyone enters through the kitchen, where Martha not only cooks but also has her office. Hers is an unforced and genuine kind of hospitality, which makes guests feel like part of the family. "I felt I could slip off my shoes and snooze by the fireplace" was one reaction. There are antiques and a handsome print of the America's Cup boat, *Defender*, but this is not a 'designer-decorated' house. Bedrooms are varied; those at the top have low ceilings and dark wood but are flooded with light from large dormer windows. Two suites in a separate cottage provide greater privacy. We like being offered a choice of breakfasts: either a full meal in the dining-room or a continental version delivered to the bedroom or favourite spot on the porch.

Nearby beaches, boating, fishing, golf, space launches.

512 South Riverside Drive, New Smyrna Beach, FL 32168
Tel (904) 423 4940
Fax (904) 427 2814
Location at S Riverside Drive and Anderson St, 2 blocks south of South Causeway; ample car parking
Meals breakfast
Prices rooms $-$$$ with breakfast
Rooms 8 double; all have bath or shower, air-conditioning, phone, TV
Facilities dining-room, sitting-room; porches, garden, dockage
Smoking outdoors only
Credit cards AE, MC, V
Children over 12
Disabled 1 adapted room
Closed never
Languages English only
Proprietors Charles and Martha Nighswonger

Central East

Waterside hotel, New Smyrna Beach

Riverview Hotel

The hotel gets its name from the view of Indian River. Standing by the North Causeway, it was built in 1885 for the bridge-tender to live in. Despite its age, however, there are no creaky floors. The 'restoration' by owners Jim and Christa Kelsey was more than just a coat of paint; it was a substantial rebuilding job, from basement to roof. The result is so tidy it looks almost brand-new: little sense of its history remains. Bedrooms, on either side of the corridors, are more 'hotel' than 'home'-style and cheery-enough, with tropical-looking prints.

Not everyone enjoys the communal eating of bed-and-breakfasts; here, your order is brought to your room 'when you like' from Riverview Charlie's, the restaurant next door. Jolly and informal, it is a typical Florida waterside spot. The hotel would suit active types who can swim in the pool, play tennis and golf nearby, and borrow bicycles to take to the beach where riding on the hard-packed sand is allowed. Don't be put off by the unappealing display of merchandise in the gift shop-cum-reception area. This is the only fault our inspector could find in what is otherwise a tempting place for a vacation.

Nearby beaches, boating, fishing, golf, space launches.

103 Flagler Avenue, New Smyrna Beach, FL 32169
Tel (904) 428 5858; (800) 945 7416
Fax (904) 423 8927
Location on east bank of Intracoastal Waterway; ample car parking
Meals breakfast, lunch, dinner
Prices rooms $-$$$ with breakfast
Rooms 18 double; all have bath or shower, air-conditioning, phone, TV, safe
Facilities restaurant; porches, swimming-pool, dockage
Smoking permitted
Credit cards AE, MC, V
Children very welcome
Disabled not suitable
Closed never
Languages English only
Proprietors Jim and Christa Kelsey

Central East

Bed-and-breakfast, North Hutchinson Island

Mellon Patch Inn

North Hutchinson Island runs from Ft Pierce to Sebastian but the inn is at the southern end of the island. Our Florida-based inspectors recommend this spot because there are few tourists but three parks that preserve Florida as it used to be. One is close enough for early-morning nature walks.

Purpose-built as a bed-and-breakfast by Andrea and Arthur Mellon in 1994, the expansive deck at the back overlooks a canal. This leads to the Indian River, the broad Intracoastal Waterway between the island and the mainland, much used by boaters. Guests who borrow the Mellons' canoe can explore the native mangroves just a short paddle away.

Bedrooms follow individual themes, with furniture and walls decorated by a local artist. Tropical fish and shells adorn 'Seaside Serenity', which has a private deck, while the larger 'Santa Fe Sunset', with deeper colours, offers the best view of the canal. Breakfast is a communal affair, served at 9 am and the cookies put out for afternoon tea are highly-rated. Unfortunately, there is no swimming-pool. Vero Beach, known for shopping, restaurants, art galleries and theatre, is a 20-minute drive away.

Nearby Vero Beach, water sports, fishing.

3601 North A1A, North Hutchinson Island, FL 34949
Tel (407) 461 5231; (800) 656 7824
Fax (407) 464 6463
Location on rte A1A on North Hutchinson Island; ample car parking
Meals breakfast, afternoon snack
Prices rooms $$ breakfast
Rooms 4 double; all have bath or shower, air-conditioning, phone, TV
Facilities dining-room, sitting-room; deck, garden, canoe
Smoking outdoors only
Credit cards AE, MC, V
Children over 12
Disabled 1 adapted room
Closed never
Languages some French
Proprietors Andrea and Arthur Mellon

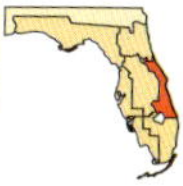

Central East

Modern bed-and-breakfast, Sebastian

The Davis House Inn

In most guide books to Florida, the map looks rather empty of sights between Vero Beach and Melbourne, but there is Sebastian Inlet, known for surfing and fishing plus the state-run recreation area of sandy beaches, mangroves and wildlife. All that, however, is on a barrier island separated from the mainland by the Indian River Intracoastal Waterway. Sebastian itself, once the only river port between Miami and St Augustine has, despite this former importance, escaped the attentions of developers. They have bypassed the area and the town retains the 'old Florida' spirit.

The inn was built in 1991 by golf fan Steven Wild, who patterned it after the clubhouse at Augusta National, Georgia, home of the US Masters Tournament. Our inspector liked the setting, with views of the waterway from the many decks, the South Seas-style Tiki bar and the Gathering Room used for breakfast or socializing. Bedrooms are modern and simple but spotlessly clean; mattresses feel firm. This is an unpretentious place, whose keen prices make it a tempting base for boaters, fishermen and golfers. Three courses are within a 10-minute drive; the state recreation area and Vero Beach are 20 minutes away.

Nearby beaches, fishing, golf, surfing, Vero Beach.

607 Davis Street, Sebastian, FL 32958
Tel (407) 589 4114
Location on Intracoastal Waterway, in small town; ample car parking
Meals breakfast
Prices rooms $-$$ with breakfast
Rooms 12 double; all have bath or shower, air-conditioning, phone, TV
Facilities dining-room, bar; decks
Smoking permitted
Credit cards MC, V
Children very welcome
Disabled 1 adapted room
Closed never
Languages English only
Proprietor Steven Wild

More on page 172

Northwest

Luxury bed-and-breakfast, Apalachicola

Coombs House Inn

Apalachicola should be on everyone's list of special places to visit in Florida. Its natural isolation has protected it from the ravages of development: fishing boats still dock at the end of the street, homes reflect 150 years of history, T-shirt shops have yet to arrive and there is a strong sense of community. Built in 1905 as a lumber baron's home, the inn is a tribute both to turn-of-the-century craftsmen and to Lynn Wilson, the current owner, whose design firm has furnished many luxury hotels in the USA. 'Studied elegance' is one reaction to the rich panelling, perfectly-chosen art, period European and American antiques and rich fabrics for curtains, chairs and beds.

In the entrance hall, the dark wood walls, ceiling and floor add up to a 'Scottish manse' look. Of the bedrooms, Coombs, has a regal king-sized bed with a subtle motif of Angels while Tupelo, at the front corner, is always sunny thanks to its many shades of yellow. Smaller and slightly less formal is Sandpiper. Bathrooms are a pleasing mixture of period fixtures and sparkling new tiles, with abundant towels. The on-site managers, Marilyn and Charlie Schubert, used to run a well-known inn in Vermont.

Nearby boating, fishing; beaches on St George Island.

80 Sixth Street, Apalachicola, FL 32320
Tel (904) 653 9199
Location in historic district; ample car parking
Meals breakfast
Prices rooms $-$$ with breakfast
Rooms 9 double; 2 suites; 1 cottage; all have bath or shower, air-conditioning, phone, TV; 1 Jacuzzi
Facilities dining-room, sitting-room; porch
Smoking outdoors only
Credit cards AE, MC, V
Children welcome
Disabled not suitable
Closed never
Languages English only
Managers Marilyn and Charlie Schubert

Northwest

Town hotel, Apalachicola

The Gibson Inn

Heading west on Route 98, a long bridge spans the Apalachicola River. Once on the other side, the old Gibson Inn is visible; in fact, the road splits to bypass the imposing, square hotel built in 1907 and first called the Franklin. What looks rather gruff on the outside, despite a porch 'meant for sitting on', is full of warmth and good cheer inside. At 'happy hour', the bar buzzes with an interesting mix of local business people and fishermen from the docks across the street. Paintings of ships at sea and stormy oceans add to the ambience. The downstairs restaurant features ocean-cold seafood favourites such as grouper Rockefeller and Apalachicola oysters. Helpings are generous. A 'potato lunch' is a baked potato stuffed with shrimp, crab, onion and mushrooms.

Bedrooms are all similar in size but come in different colours. A quiet room at the back, Number 204, has green woodwork, a white iron bed and a red and white bathroom. Number 307 offers views of the river and the bridge but number 304 is special for its blue quilted canopy bed, a fine armoire and, for contrast, a modern framed print. We were impressed by the friendly, helpful staff who set a relaxed style in this relatively large, busy inn.
Nearby fishing fleet, historic village walks, beaches.

51 Avenue C, Apalachicola, FL 32320
Tel (904) 653 2191
Location by the river in heart of town; ample car parking
Meals breakfast, lunch, dinner
Prices rooms $-$$ with breakfast
Rooms 27 double; 3 suites; all have bath or shower, air-conditioning, phone, TV
Facilities dining-room, sitting-room, bar
Smoking permitted
Credit cards AE, MC, V
Children very welcome
Disabled not suitable
Closed never
Languages English only
Proprietors Michael and Neil Koun and Michael Merlo

Northwest

Island bed-and-breakfast, Cedar Key

Cedar Key Bed-and-Breakfast

Cedar Key is one of a cluster of small islands that lack the long white beaches of tourist board posters. This has saved them from over-development and several are now nature reserves. Once over the causeway from the mainland, there are no traffic lights, no cinema and no fast food. Among the 800 permanent residents are many from out-of-state,.such as Lois and Bob Davenport. They were high school sweethearts in Indiana but their paths diverged until a class reunion brought them together after 30 years. Fate also dictated a new lifestyle. "We didn't prepare for innkeeping, we just did it." That was in 1995.

Now their 115-year old yellow-pine house is furnished prettily but simply. The gramophone and domed clock are old but not museum-quality; lace curtains look pleasingly old-fashioned rather than precious against painted walls and floors. "This was not a wealthy home, it was built as a boarding house," so rooms are modestly-sized. The centuries-old live oaks in the garden are, however, magnificent. Guests play croquet or borrow the kayak and bicycles. These hosts are down-to-earth but not too serious: there may be Mickey Mouse waffles for breakfast.

Nearby uninhabited islands, nature reserves, boating, beaches.

PO Box 700, Cedar Key, FL 32625
Tel (352) 543 9000; (800) 453 5051
Fax (352) 543 8070
Location corner of 3rd and F Streets in quiet residential district; own car parking
Meals breakfast, afternoon snack
Prices rooms $-$$ with breakfast
Rooms 7 double; all have bath or shower, air-conditioning
Facilities dining-room; porch, garden, bicycles, kayak
Smoking outdoors only
Credit cards AE, MC, V
Children over 10
Disabled access to 1 room
Closed first two weeks Dec
Languages English only
Proprietors Lois and Bob Davenport

Northwest

Island hotel, Cedar Key

Island Hotel

"When I told my family I was buying a hotel in Florida, they imagined a concrete block, not an inn dating back to 1859." English-born Alison Sanders and her American husband, Tom, bought the place in 1992 and restored only where necessary. The Neptune Bar, for example, needed rebuilding in order to reclaim its former title of 'local haunt'. Having known the hotel for years, Tom was determined to preserve its 'eccentric' character. So, floors still slope and creak, screen doors slam and rooms lack telephones and televisions. Instead, guests play chess or take books or old magazines to read on the upstairs wrap-around porch. Furniture throughout is old and comfortable, decoration is plain but with some style. In Number 23 the bathtub is in the bedroom, while in Number 36, a mosquito net drapes the bed and large Mexican tiles completely cover the bathroom.

The restaurant deserves its fine reputation for locally-caught crabs, oysters, clams and fish. The tomato-basil soup is 'honest and tasty', poppy-seed bread arrives warm and butter is in a little pot, not wrapped in foil. Many first-time guests book for one night but stay on, seduced by the 'laid-back' atmosphere here.
Nearby uninhabited islands, nature reserves, boating, beaches.

PO Box 460, Cedar Key, FL 32625
Tel (352) 543 5111
Location in heart of town, on 3rd Street, between A and B Streets; own car parking
Meals breakfast, dinner
Prices rooms $$ breakfast
Rooms 10 double; 6 have bath or shower; all have air-conditioning
Facilities 2 dining-rooms, sitting-room, bar; courtyard bar, porch
Smoking restricted
Credit cards AE, MC, V
Children over 10
Disabled not suitable
Closed never; restaurant only, Tuesday
Languages some French, Japanese
Proprietors Alison and Tom Sanders

Northwest

Bed-and-breakfast, DeFuniak Springs

Sunbright Manor

Once the railroad reached this corner of Florida's Western Panhandle in 1882, winter visitors began to discover the almost circular spring-fed lake. Imposing homes were built in the forest of yellow pines and, in 1885, the New York Chautauqua, an educational institute aimed at the self-improvement of adults, opened a palatial winter headquarters here. This auditorium, complete with lecture rooms, dates from 1909 and, despite hurricane damage, still looks grander than many state capitol buildings. The revived Chautauqua Festival is held each spring.

DeFuniak Springs' century-old houses sport fluted columns, window dormers, and turrets. Sunbright Manor is no exception, with 33 columns and 1600 spindles along the double-decker verandas overlooking a relatively busy intersection. The high-ceiling rooms are filled with unremarkable turn-of-the-century furnishings. What brings the house to life is the energy of Byrdie Mitchell who leads daytime tours of her home which also has a small antiques and collectibles shop. After coffee in their rooms, overnight guests meet at 8 am in the formal dining-room for a serious breakfast: fruit soups, muffins, cheese and sausage soufflés.

Nearby historic houses, Chautauqua, lake.

30 Live Oak Avenue,
DeFuniak Springs, FL 32433
Tel (904) 892 0656
Location corner of Live Oak Ave and Highway 331; ample car parking
Meals breakfast
Prices rooms $ with breakfast
Rooms 3 double; two have bath or shower; all have air-conditioning; 1 hot tub
Facilities dining-room, sitting-room; verandas, garden
Smoking not permitted
Credit cards V
Children not suitable
Disabled not suitable
Closed never
Languages English only
Proprietors John and Byrdie Mitchell

Northwest

Beach-side inn, Destin

Henderson Park Inn

Of Florida's 1,100 miles (1,760 km) of sandy beaches, the Gulf shores of the Panhandle are arguably the least well-known. Although hundreds of motels and condominiums line the coast between the Alabama border and Apalachee Bay, the Henderson Park Inn is the only small hotel we found that can truly claim to be right on the beach. White sand and sea oats are all around, while the neighbouring State park ensures protection from the tide of modern development.

This part of Florida is thin on historic beach houses, so the building itself comes as a surprise. Its green roofs, shingled walls and white trim are classic images of coastal Maine. Although it looks old, it was built in 1992 by Bill Abbott, who wanted to recreate the sort of traditional New England hotel where he and his father had once worked. The bedrooms, filled with antique and reproduction furniture, are named after French Impressionist painters. Monet is the most popular.

This is no hideaway: guests meet for cocktails round the swimming-pool and locals use the Veranda restaurant, so the atmosphere is sociable. Fifteen more bedrooms are planned.

Nearby Henderson State Recreation area; beach, fishing, golf.

2700 Old Beach Highway 98, Destin, FL 32541
Tel (904) 654 0400; (800) 336 4853
Fax (904) 654 0405
Location in quiet cul-de-sac; ample car parking
Meals breakfast, lunch, dinner, snacks
Prices rooms $$-$$$$ with breakfast
Rooms 20 double (35 in 1997); all have bath or shower, Jacuzzi, air-conditioning, phone, TV, refrigerator, safe
Facilities swimming-pool
Smoking permitted; not in restaurant
Credit cards AE, MC, V
Children very welcome
Disabled 1 room adapted
Closed never; restaurant only, Sun eve, Mon
Languages Spanish
Manager Susie Nunnerly

Northwest

Downtown hotel, Pensacola

New World Inn

Restored wrought-iron balconies give a New Orleans French Quarter look to Pensacola's historic district, which is being enthusiastically renewed. Now museums, boutiques and art centres complement professional offices in an area that was water when the Spanish arrived in 1559. Over the centuries, sailing ships dumped so much ballast that a finger of land has been reclaimed. Also reclaimed is the New World Inn, once a box factory, where exposed brickwork and an industrial-looking roof line recall the past. Now it is part of a restaurant and conference hall complex just two blocks from the bay.

In the cool, dark wood-panelled lobby, an unobtrusive line-up of celebrity guest photographs overlooks old model ships. Bedrooms are attractive, comfortable and business-like rather than imaginative, with reproduction four poster beds. In the high-ceilinged Pensacola dining room, the emphasis is on 'fish' and 'fresh': Shrimp Dolores echoes New Orleans, with a *rémoulade* sauce. The Liverpool Pub, as the name implies, aims for a British pub ambience. The owners are gradually increasing the 'plush factor' by upgrading carpets, quilts and curtains.

Nearby Pensacola Auditorium, Historic District, art centre.

600 South Palafox Street, Pensacola, FL 32501
Tel (904) 432 4111
Location in downtown, revived port area; ample car parking
Meals breakfast, lunch, dinner
Prices rooms $-$$$ with breakfast
Rooms 14 double; 2 suites; all have bath or shower, air-conditioning, phone, TV
Facilities 3 dining-rooms, sitting-room, bar
Smoking permitted
Credit cards AE, DC, MC, V
Children over 6
Disabled not suitable
Closed never; restaurant, Sun, Mon
Languages English only
Manager Janice Sheehan

Northwest

Bed-and-breakfast, Quincy

McFarlin House

When the Fauble family bought the house in 1994, it was a near-ruin after standing empty for 20 years. Luckily, Richard Fauble is experienced in renovations and tackled the project with gusto. One year on, new plumbing and wiring, central heating and air-conditioning had been installed. Even more impressive is the exemplary restoration of the curly pine woodwork, fireplaces and moulding, let alone the stunning fretwork screen originally made by a French craftsmen. Overall, rooms are large, with fine windows and high ceilings where fans spin slowly, reflecting the unhurried pace of life in this part of Florida. The Turret Bedroom, with its curved walls, is a favourite, as are the two top floor bedrooms with their steeply-pitched roof lines. The 'better-than-average' Victorian furnishings are sparingly placed, and do not detract from the architectural details.

Only 20 minutes north of Tallahassee, Quincy is known for its Historic District. East King Street is quiet, much as it must have been in 1895 when tobacco planter John McFarlin built his spacious home with its parade of 42 pillars. He would be pleased to see the condition it is in today.

Nearby antiques shops, Historic District.

305 East King Street, Quincy, FL 32351
Tel (904) 875 2526
Location corner of Love and King Streets; ample car parking
Meals breakfast
Prices rooms $$ with breakfast
Rooms 9 double; 7 have bath or shower; all have air-conditioning
Facilities dining-room, 2 sitting-rooms; veranda, garden
Smoking outdoors only
Credit cards AE, DC, MC, V
Children very welcome
Disabled access 1 room
Closed never
Languages English only
Proprietors Richard and Tina Fauble

Northwest

Beach hotel, St George Island

St George Inn

St George Island, the largest of the Gulf of Mexico barrier islands, is connected by bridge and causeway to the mainland yet retains a remoteness that satisfies those wanting to get away from it all. Barbara Vail and her late husband Jack, built the large square white hotel in 1986 and she continues to run it almost single-handedly.

The Gulf is only a couple of minutes' walk in one direction, Apalachicola Bay a few minutes in another, so most guests are content to be beach vacationers. Plain, simple and unpretentious, all rooms have water views and open on to the wrap-around porches.

The surprise comes in the dining-room. This is the domain of chef Cole Nelson, who trained at the Culinary Institute of America and also worked in Paris. He serves up the freshest of seafood: an excellent bouillabaisse followed by oven-roasted grouper with tomato and fennel or pan-seared shrimp and scallop pasta.

Prices here are attractive, particularly when compared to better-known seaside places further south. Remember, though, that mosquitoes can be a problem for delicate skins at certain times of the year.

Nearby Apalachicola, St George State Park, beaches.

HCR Box 222, Franklin Boulevard, St George Island, FL 32328
Tel (904) 927 2903
Location Franklin Blvd and Pine St; ample car parking
Meals breakfast, dinner
Prices rooms $-$$ with breakfast
Rooms 8 double; all have bath or shower, air-conditioning, TV
Facilities dining-room, sitting-room; veranda
Smoking not permitted
Credit cards MC, V
Children over 12
Disabled not suitable
Closed never
Languages English only
Proprietor Barbara Vail

Northwest

Bed-and-breakfast, Santa Rosa Beach

A Highlands House

The beaches of South Walton run all along the Gulf of Mexico close to Florida's westernmost shoreline border with Alabama. Accommodation consisted mainly of condominiums and motels when Joan and Ray Robins' took the bold decision to open the first bed-and-breakfast in the area. That was in 1991; since then, holidaymakers from all over the world have stayed in the custom-designed Caribbean-style bungalow. Wicker chairs stand on the wide veranda; inside are green carpeting, white walls and pickled wood furniture.

Don't expect a water view: the location is one row of houses and two minutes' walk away from the renowned sandy beach. This is a family-style bed-and-breakfast but with a business-like approach. Joan is a spirited, optimistic hostess who bounced back after Hurricane Opal hit the area hard late in 1995. Her breakfast repertoire runs to 37 dishes. The benefits of a new building include modern, central air-conditioning and efficient bathrooms but the overall feel is rather impersonal, albeit pleasant and comfortable. The carriage house behind offers more privacy. The dog, Teddy, is cute but can be over-eager.

Nearby beaches, fishing, some golf.

PO Box 1189, 10 Bullard Road, Santa Rosa Beach, FL 32459
Tel (904) 267 0110
Fax (904) 267 3602
Location off route 30A in Beach Highlands Area, Dune Allen Beach; ample car parking
Meals breakfast
Prices rooms $$-$$ with breakfast
Rooms 3 double; 1 suite; all have bath or shower, air-conditioning
Facilities dining-room, sitting-room
Smoking not permitted
Credit cards MC, V
Children very welcome
Disabled not suitable
Closed never
Languages English only
Proprietors Joan and Ray Robins

Northwest

Gulf shore inn, Seaside

Josephine's

Like a Hollywood set, the resort town of Seaside was constructed in 1981 on one of the world's best silver sand beaches. Houses are painted in sorbet shades with differences in detail for variety. Picket fences and brick streets, pools and a gazebo add up to an attractive, if slightly unreal whole, which is, nevertheless, hugely popular.

Josephine's dates from 1990 but its stately proportions recall pre-Civil War Southern mansions. The sure touch of an interior decorator shows in the co-ordinated fabrics and prints. American and European antiques lend a sense of age and even bathrooms follow the conceit, with old tubs surrounded by gleaming new marble and antique-looking taps concealing efficient plumbing. The bonus is the restaurant where Bruce Albert updates Southern standards such as fried green tomatoes and key lime pie and veers to the trendy with wild mesclun salads or grilled vegetables. The wine list is short but well-chosen. Since the Alberts 'grew up in the hotel business', there is a welcome professionalism throughout. This inn would thrive anywhere; combined with its world-class beach, it is a winner.

Nearby beach, concerts, shopping, dining.

101 Seaside Avenue, PO Box 4767, Seaside, FL 32459
Tel (904) 231 1940; (800) 848 1840
Location on quiet street, near hub of town; ample car parking
Meals breakfast, lunch, dinner
Prices rooms $$$-$$$$ with breakfast
Rooms 7 double; 4 suites; all have bath or shower, air-conditioning, phone, TV, refrigerator, some fireplaces
Facilities dining-room, sitting-room
Smoking outdoors only
Credit cards MC, V
Children welcome
Disabled suitable, 1 adapted room
Closed never
Languages English only
Proprietors Judy and Bruce Albert

Northwest

Resort hotel, Steinhatchee

Steinhatchee Landing

Far away from it all, west of Route 19, the area near the mouth of the Steinhatchee River has long been a happy hunting-ground for sportsmen in search of deer, wild boar, turkey and duck. Former US President Jimmy Carter once had a home down here. In 1990, a company opened Steinhatchee (pronounced STEEN-hatchy) Landing, a complex of 20 self-catering cottages built to recreate a late Victorian atmosphere just inland from the Gulf of Mexico. Palm trees and foot bridges, moss oaks and fishing piers have all been woven into the landscaping so that each wood-framed cottage looks and feels secluded.

Do not expect the personal touch of an innkeeper here. We include this small resort because it is ideal for families, particularly those with energetic children. Although popular with boaters, the sports facilities range from archery to tennis and from canoeing to volleyball, all included in the price.

Although each cottage has a kitchen, breakfast is delivered and a short walk away is The Landing's Restaurant, open to the public. Remember that there is a two-night minimum stay at weekends, three nights for major holidays.
Nearby fishing, boating, beach.

PO Box 789, Steinhatchee, FL 32359
Tel (352) 498 3513
Fax (352) 498 2346
Location on Route 51, 8 miles (13 km) west of Route 19; ample car parking
Meals breakfast
Prices rooms $$-$$$$
Rooms 20 cottages; all have bath or shower, air-conditioning, phone, TV, kitchen
Facilities The Landing's Restaurant; garden, spa, outdoor swimming-pool, bicycles, canoes, playground, tennis courts
Smoking outdoors only
Credit cards AE, DC, MC, V
Children very welcome
Disabled not suitable
Closed never
Languages Spanish
Manager Dean Fowler

Northwest

City hotel, Tallahassee

Governors Inn

Tallahassee is the state capital of Florida and right in the middle of the city, perched on a hilltop, stands the Capitol complex. Half a block away is the Governors Inn, whose awning over the main entrance provides the only clue that this is an hotel among the line of brick façades along Adams Street.

Inside, wood is a feature. In the entrance, the exposed structural heart-of-pine timbering creates contemporary geometrical patterns while, on the right, pale pine panels the high-ceilinged Florida Room, which serves as both breakfast-room and bar. Bedrooms are similar, business-like and named for former governors such as Spessard Holland. Antiques such as rock maple cupboards and black oak writing desks are mixed with reproductions. With 40 rooms, this is no hideaway and, not surprisingly, the working week is busy with a predominance of corporate suits and ties. A weekend football game would bring cheerful T-shirted alumni of Florida State University to enliven what is otherwise a quiet time for strolling through the Historic District. The Andrews 2nd Act restaurant across the street, open for lunch and dinner, offers room service to hotel guests.

Nearby Capitol, downtown shopping.

209 South Adams Street, Tallahassee, FL 32301
Tel (904) 681 6855; (800) 342 7717 (FL)
Fax (904) 222 3105
Location in heart of city; valet car parking
Meals breakfast
Prices rooms $$-$$$$ with breakfast
Rooms 32 double; 8 suites; all have bath or shower, air-conditioning, phone, TV, radio; 1 whirlpool tub
Facilities sitting-room, bar
Smoking permitted
Credit cards AE, DC, MC, V
Children very welcome
Disabled not suitable
Closed never
Languages English only
Manager Charles Orr

Riverside fishing lodge, Yankeetown

Izaak Walton Lodge

Europeans are constantly surprised by the traditions from the Old World that live on in the New. Who would expect a lodge in the middle of nowhere to be dedicated to the famous Englishman who, over 300 years ago, wrote the quintessential treatise on angling? Yet, A F Knotts, who put up this rambling building on the Withlacoochee River, was a fisherman who wanted to bring like-minded friends down from the North to enjoy this unspoiled, heavily-wooded part of Florida, just inland from the Gulf.

That was back in 1922, but Yankeetown remains a hamlet of 20 houses and a fire station, where fishermen return with tales of the sheephead or catfish that got away and locals take osprey and alligators for granted. In the spacious wood lodge, bedrooms have been redecorated but are still plain and simple, with separate bathrooms down the hall for men and women.

This all adds up to a genuine Old Florida experience - with one major exception. Few fishing lodges anywhere can boast a proper restaurant serving Châteaubriand or smoked boar with rosemary sauce. Diners drive from as far away as St Petersburg to enjoy Jim Brauer's cooking and panoramic views of the river.

Nearby Gulf of Mexico, fishing, boating, nature reserves.

1 63rd Street, Yankeetown, FL 34498
Tel (352) 447 2311
Fax (352) 447 3264
Location turn off at junction of 63rd Street and Riverside Drive; ample car parking
Meals breakfast, lunch, dinner
Prices rooms $-$$ with breakfast
Rooms 9 double; 2 cottages; 7 share bath or shower; some with air-conditioning
Facilities 2 dining-rooms, sitting-room; porch, garden
Smoking restricted
Credit cards AE, MC, V
Children welcome
Disabled not suitable
Closed Monday
Languages English only
Proprietors Jim Brauer, Wayne and Linda Harrington

More on page 173

Northeast

Bed-and-breakfast, Amelia Island

The Addison House

'Unlike any bed-and-breakfast or inn I have ever seen' was our well-travelled inspector's reaction to what he describes as 'an artistic statement, deserving a report in *Architectural Digest*'.

The 160-year old wood frame house is normal in shape, but painted a bright blue. Inside, rooms are mere backdrops to a selection of beautiful objects. "I don't like clutter", owner Melodie Winston's understated explanation, is exemplified by the entrance, furnished with just one tall gilt mirror and a handsome Empire table. She loves French and Italian antiques but has placed just one perfect French empire chair in the sitting-room.

The unusual charcoal grey colour of the dining-room sets off the black and white photographs of her daughter, and an eye-catching modern table. Upstairs, the Shaker bedroom, a collage of black and white, contrasts with the shocking lavender of its large, modern bathroom.

Melodie herself is unaffectedly modest about her creation. This is not an inn for everyone, however. It is 'a challenge to chintz and lace sensibilities but a memorable experience' for anyone interested in design and ready for something different.

Nearby beaches, golf, tennis, boating.

614 Ash Street, Amelia Island, FL 32034
Tel (904) 277 1604
Location Fernandina Beach, northern Amelia Island; car parking on street
Meals breakfast
Prices rooms $$-$$$$ with breakfast
Rooms 2 double; all have bath or shower, air-conditioning; 1 Jacuzzi
Facilities dining-room, 2 sitting-rooms
Smoking not permitted
Credit cards not accepted
Children not suitable
Disabled not suitable
Closed never
Languages English only
Proprietors Melodie Winston

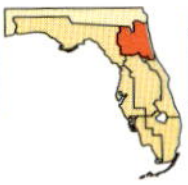

Northeast

Luxury inn, Amelia Island

Amelia Island Williams House

Even the most sophisticated visitors are awed by their first visit to this opulent, elegant 140-year old mansion which one guest described as 'a private museum complete with Oriental and European art and antiques'. Certainly, few bed-and-breakfasts anywhere can boast of a series of Japanese prints on silk, commissioned by an emperor in 1597, a carpet that was owned by Napoleon or the last Emperor of China's robe. Owner Dick Flitz would lovingly describe every item (much of the Napoleonic memorabilia is from his ancestors) but thoughtfully and thankfully, written histories of the treasures are in each guest room, to be studied at leisure.

The Empress Eugenie Suite, often used for newly-weds, has a rare Champagne glass mantelpiece and an 1850s French camelback bed. Not surprisingly, breakfast is served on china, with crystal glasses and sterling silver cutlery. The exterior detail is equally impressive: wrap-around verandas, a Victorian garden and a courtyard complete with fountain. A neighbouring property has recently been acquired and renovated, adding four more luxurious bedrooms including a second lavish Bridal Suite.
Nearby town, shopping, walking, beach, sports.

103 South 9th Street,
Fernandina Beach, FL 32034
Tel (904) 277 2328
Location Historic District, northern Amelia Island; ample car parking
Meals breakfast
Prices rooms $$-$$$ with breakfast
Rooms 8 double; all have bath or shower, air-conditioning, phone, TV; 1 Jacuzzi
Facilities dining-room, sitting-room; porch, garden
Smoking outdoors only
Credit cards MC, V
Children over 12
Disabled not suitable
Closed never
Languages English only
Proprietors Dick Flitz and Chris Carter

Northeast

Bed-and-breakfast, Amelia Island

The Bailey House

The family that built the house and gave it its name lived here from 1895 to 1963. The plans, which visitors can still see, were mail-ordered from Tennessee and implemented by local boat builders. When Tom and Jenny Bishop moved in in 1993, they were keen to revive the Victorian ambience, so Tiffany-style stained glass abounds in the entrance and up the stairs. In the main sitting-room stands an elaborate rococo revival love seat that looks like a huge butterfly. Heart-of-pine floors and half-a-dozen fireplaces add to the effect. The Amelia bedroom, with its separate entrance and wheelchair access, is the largest room. All the antique beds have firm, new mattresses. If there is a weak link, it must be the bathrooms which are a little too Victorian for some visitors' liking with restricted space for shaving kit and showers shoe-horned into odd little spaces.

The owners are new to the bed-and-breakfast business but what they lack in knowledge and experience they make up for in effort. Bicycles are useful for exploring the Historic District, while the excellent Beech Street Grill, only 2 minutes' walk away, is well-recommended for dinner.

Nearby beaches; fishing, golf, tennis; town strolling.

28 South 7th Street, PO Box 805, Fernandina Beach, FL 32035
Tel (904) 261 5390; (800) 251 5390
Location on quiet street in Historic District; car parking on street
Meals breakfast
Prices rooms $$ with breakfast
Rooms 5 double; all have bath or shower, air-conditioning, phone, TV
Facilities dining-room, 2 sitting-rooms; veranda, garden, bicycles
Smoking outdoors only
Credit cards AE, MC, V
Children over 8
Disabled suitable, 1 adapted room
Closed never
Languages English only
Proprietors Tom and Jenny Bishop

Northeast

New inn, Amelia Island

Elizabeth Pointe Lodge

Just a few steps from the white sands of the island's Atlantic Beach, the first impression is of a New England-style beach house, with weathered grey shingles. The Caple family, who used to run the nearby 1735 House, built this inn in 1992. Although there is a brisk professionalism at the front desk, the rest of the house is aimed at relaxation.

Inside are window seats and books; outside, rocking chairs on wide porches and sun loungers on the dunes. In winter, guests sit by the log fire in the gaping fieldstone fireplace and watch the Atlantic breakers. The sunrise views are spectacular.

Bedrooms are comfortable without being lavish. Four rooms have specially-made wooden Captain's beds that are built into the floor, as on board a ship, while bathrooms have big tubs for soaking. The 7 am start to breakfast suits golfers, fishermen and business travellers; at weekends, orders are taken up until 11 am, so guests can sleep late. Home-made soup, salads, sandwiches and desserts are served all day and through the evening. The combination of uncrowded, unspoiled beach with Fernandina's nearby shops and restaurant is hard to beat.

Nearby water sports, fishing, golf, tennis; Fernandina.

98 South Fletcher Avenue, Amelia Island, FL 32034
Tel (904) 277 4851
Location on the beach at north end of Amelia Island; ample car parking
Meals breakfast, light meals
Prices rooms $$-$$$$ with breakfast
Rooms 20 double; 2 cottages; all have bath or shower, air-conditioning, phone, TV; some Jacuzzi
Facilities dining-room, sitting-room, lift/elevator; porch, bicycles
Smoking outdoors only
Credit cards AE, MC, V
Children welcome
Disabled 1 adapted room
Closed never
Languages English only
Manager Helen Cook

Northeast

Bed-and-breakfast, Amelia Island

The Fairbanks House

The first impression here is memorable, thanks to the spacious garden shaded by tall, live oaks dripping with Spanish moss. This allows guests to stand back and appreciate the arched piazza windows, the soaring brick chimneys and a tower that could have been transported from Siena.

There are no disappointments inside, where most of the decoration is in tune with the Italianate villa-look: draped curtains, four poster beds, oriental carpets and gleaming hardwood floors. Rooms still have the grand fireplaces that architect Robert Schuyler designed back in 1885, but owners Mary and Nelson Smelker have made their mark by hanging a modern painting in the parlour. Each bedroom's decoration is different. Number 7 feels masculine with its regimental striped fabric; number 3, a suite with a magnificent Jacuzzi, overlooks the swimming-pool; number 6 has a fine bathroom with soapstone fixtures. Bedrooms and bathrooms are so large that visitors do not trip over their belongings. Full marks, too, for the coffee, reflecting the owners' attention to detail. There are gourmet and mystery weekends, so mid-week is quieter.

Nearby Historic District, walking, beaches, shopping, sports.

227 South 7th Street, Amelia Island, FL 32034
Tel (904) 277 0500; (800) 261 4838
Fax (904) 277 3103
Location Historic Fernandina Beach; ample car parking
Meals breakfast
Prices rooms $$-$$$ with breakfast
Rooms 8 double; 2 cottages; all have bath or shower, air-conditioning, phone, TV, hairdrier; several Jacuzzi
Facilities dining-room, sitting-room; porch, garden, outdoor swimming-pool
Smoking outdoors only
Credit cards AE, MC, V
Children welcome
Disabled not suitable
Closed never
Languages English only
Proprietors Mary and Nelson Smelker

Northeast

Bed-and-breakfast, Amelia Island

Hoyt House

Fred Hoyt, the banker who built this Queen Anne-style home at the beginning of the century, would like what he would see here today. Surrounded by well-kept lawns, the yellow building with its blue trim is framed by mature oak trees that double as insulation from the traffic on Atlantic Avenue. He would be surprised, however, by the interior, where owner Rita Kovacevich has given full vent to her creativity. Fresh flowers provide bold splashes in the plum-coloured formal dining-room. Bedrooms are named after colour schemes: Pewter, with warm greys accented by yellow and black, or Fire Coral, with an eye-catching fretwork headboard. In Sunrise Yellow, an old steamer trunk serves as the focal point. Our inspector applauded the bathrooms, 'no rattling pipes, water stains or drips, with great towels and space to put one's gear.' The Kovacevichs left New York in 1993 and insist that Hoyt House has extended their lives by 15 years because they enjoy being hosts so much. An annexe at the rear of the house has the same adventurous decoration. For some reason, unexplained by the jolly, bear-like John, guests keep adding to the collection of carved, ceramic and toy giraffes.

Nearby fishing, boating, beaches; town strolling/shopping.

804 Atlantic Avenue,
Fernandina Beach, FL 32034
Tel (904) 277 4300; (800) 432 2085
Location in Historic District; ample car parking
Meals breakfast
Prices rooms $$-$$$ with breakfast
Rooms 9 double; all have bath or shower, air-conditioning; some fireplaces; phone, TV on request;
Facilities dining-room, 3 sitting-rooms; veranda, garden, gazebo, outdoor hot tub
Smoking outdoors only
Credit cards AE, MC, V
Children over 10
Disabled not suitable
Closed never
Languages English only
Proprietors John and Rita Kovacevich

Northeast

Bed-and-breakfast, Amelia Island

The Walnford Inn

There are 'two-for-the-price-of-one' advantages to staying on this quiet corner in the Historic District of Fernandina. Two couples, the Walns and the Myers, share the innkeeping duties, which they say keeps them 'fresh and energized'. Behind the neat, white picket fence are two houses, joined by a small deck.

Inside is a comfortable balance between the old, for atmosphere, and the new, for comfort. Surprisingly, the older Guest House (1880) looks more contemporary, with wall-to-wall carpets, whirlpool tubs and plentiful cupboards. The Main House dates from 1905 and has the sort of kitchen where guests congregate. "I tried to discourage them but failed," says Ann Myers, "so I learned to listen while I cook." This informality appeals to guests who want to avoid themed weekends or over-enthusiastic hosts. Breakfast is unhurried, served on the broad porch in fine weather, or in the dining-room.

Each bedroom is different. The Solomon Room features an enormous antique mirror from New Orleans as a headboard, while the Rose Room has a black iron bed with a bright, white quilt. A two night minimum stay is required at holiday weekends.

Nearby shopping, town; beaches.

102 South 7th Street, Fernandina Beach, FL 32034
Tel (904) 277 6660; (800) 277 6660
Location in Historic District; car parking on street
Meals breakfast
Prices rooms $$ with breakfast
Rooms 7 double; all have bath or shower, air-conditioning, phone, TV; 4 Jacuzzi
Facilities dining-room, sitting-room; veranda, garden
Smoking outdoors only
Credit cards MC, V
Children over 12
Disabled not suitable
Closed never
Languages English only
Proprietors Larry and Ann Myers, Linda and Bob Waln

Northeast

Restaurant with rooms, Crescent City

Sprague House Inn

Halfway between Jacksonville and Orlando, the region at the northern end of Florida's lake district is quiet and rural. Hilly farmland and clear, freshwater lakes give it a New England atmosphere. Built in 1892, the Steamboat Gothic-style inn was a stopover for the river traffic that shipped citrus fruit across Crescent Lake to the St John's River.

Much of the original stained and etched glass survives, as do the tall, live oaks outside. However, the Moyers do not live in the past. "This is a fun place to visit," according to guests who are intrigued by the vast collection of stuffed animals. The challenge is to spot everything in alphabetical order from armadillo to zebra. The animal theme continues in the bedrooms. Number 5 has a red fox by the bed, a tarpon on the wall and a lynx rug underfoot. All are spacious with four poster beds, big windows and access to the upper porch. Bathrooms are large and comfortable.

The pub-style restaurant is Terry's domain. Seafood and steaks are the speciality with hot crab dip and hot peach cobbler enthusiastically endorsed. 'A great find in a relatively undiscovered part of the state,' decided our inspector.

Nearby Crescent Lake, boating, fishing, Ocala National Forest.

125 Central Avenue, Crescent City, FL 32112
Tel (904) 698 2430
Location on Rte 17, on the shore of Crescent Lake; ample car parking
Meals breakfast, lunch, dinner
Prices rooms $-$$$ with breakfast
Rooms 3 double; 3 suites; all have bath or shower, air-conditioning, TV
Facilities 2 dining-rooms, sitting-room; garden, bicycles
Smoking only in restaurant
Credit cards MC, V
Children not suitable
Disabled not suitable
Closed never
Languages English only
Proprietors Terry and Vena Moyer

Northeast

Historic bed-and-breakfast, Gainesville

Magnolia Plantation

In 1995, the annual survey by *Money* magazine of the 'best places to live in the USA' ranked Gainesville number one. Luckily, locals had changed the name back in 1853 to honour General Gaines; otherwise, Hogtown would have been in the top slot. Whatever the name, this attractive city is known as the home of the University of Florida. Traditional neighbourliness survives here: when Joe and Cindy Montalto bought the dilapidated, 1885-built house and started renovations, 'people just showed up on our doorstep, wanting to help.'

Now, the original wood floors and mahogany banister shine with polish, while antiques include a handsome carved cherry bed in Gardenia, the bridal chamber complete with family wedding portraits. Other mementoes range from Cindy's christening dress to a portrait of Joe's grandmother. The family, however is more than a decorating theme; Cindy's mother, Beth Turner, helps with the innkeeping and Joe's father landscaped the garden. The friendly, almost folksy ambience would suit those who enjoy getting to know their hosts. Bathrooms, however, can be small, while in Azalea, the bathtub stands in the bedroom.

Nearby University of Florida, botanical gardens, lakes.

309 SE Seventh Street,
Gainesville, FL 32601
Tel (352) 375 6653
Location on quiet street in residential area; own car parking
Meals breakfast, afternoon snack
Prices rooms $-$$ with breakfast
Rooms 5 double; 1 cottage; all have bath or shower, air-conditioning, radio
Facilities dining-room, 2 sitting-rooms; porch, garden
Smoking outdoors only
Credit cards MC, V
Children welcome
Disabled not suitable
Closed never
Languages English only
Proprietors Joe and Cindy Montalto

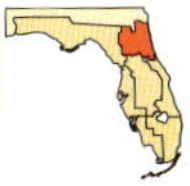

Northeast

City bed-and-breakfast, Gainesville

Sweetwater Branch Inn

A well-known place to stay, the inn is part of a larger business. Bedrooms in the 1885-built Cushman-Colson House are often booked for guests at the meetings and weddings held next door in the larger, grander McKenzie House. Brides no doubt pose for photographs under the wisteria-covered trellis or on the bridge leading to a pretty garden. The office is in the Carriage House at the back. Those staying at the Cushman-Colson House enter through the large kitchen, whose modernity contrasts with the old-fashioned flavour of the rest of the building. Bedrooms are understated but attractive, perhaps with fireplaces, lace curtains and carved or canopied beds. Those at the back overlooking the courtyard and fountain are the most quiet, since University Avenue is a busy thoroughfare.

We would not chose this for a romantic weekend away from it all. It seems more suited to visitors touring in the region, or those in the city for meetings, such as the businessman we saw working on his portable computer. Instead of the usual muffins, juice and coffee, breakfasts here include pancakes or eggs cooked to order, anytime from 7.30-9.30 am.

Nearby University of Florida, botanical gardens, lakes.

625 East University Avenue, Gainesville, FL 32601
Tel (352) 373 6760; (800) 451 7111
Fax (352) 371 3771
Location on busy main street not far from downtown; own car parking
Meals breakfast, afternoon snack
Prices rooms $-$$ with breakfast
Rooms 4 double; 3 suites; all have bath or shower, air-conditioning, phone, radio; TV by request
Facilities dining-room, sitting-room; porch, garden
Smoking outdoors only
Credit cards AE, MC, V
Children very welcome
Disabled access to 3 rooms
Closed never
Languages Italian
Proprietor Cornelia Holbrook

Northeast

Town bed-and-breakfast, High Springs

Grady House

The area northwest of Gainesville may be inland from Florida's famous beaches, but it is a regional holiday destination thanks to the crystal clear natural springs and rivers that attract swimmers and canoeists. The village of High Springs is known for antiques shops. Built in 1917 as a bakery, the house became a boarding-house and then a family home. It was bought in 1990 by Diane and Ed Shupe, who "used to bicycle past. I kept saying it had potential; Ed would ignore me and ride on."

Three years' renovation resulted in a homey, comfortable place to stay. The decoration is "what we like". That means prints of Old Masters and 20thC artists plus old iron beds and claw-foot bath-tubs. Four of the five bedrooms have an additional sitting-room but some bathrooms are tiny. With shelves of books, a thought for the day on a blackboard and classical music playing, we assumed that the Shupes were quiet and serious. Then we saw the delightfully whimsical Cinnamon Room. This is the honeymoon suite, covered with 35 prints of female nudes, though, for the sake of equality, there are a few male nudes in the bathroom, where the bathtub is big enough for two.

Nearby Ichetucknee Springs State Park, shopping.

420 NW First Avenue, PO Box 205, High Springs, FL 32643
Tel (904) 454 2206
Location on a main street in town; public car parking on street
Meals breakfast
Prices rooms $-$$ with breakfast
Rooms 1 double; 4 suites; all have bath or shower, air-conditioning, radio
Facilities dining-room, sitting-room; porch, garden
Smoking outdoors only
Credit cards MC, V
Children over 8
Disabled not suitable
Closed never
Languages English only
Proprietors Ed and Diane Shupe

Northeast

Country retreat, High Springs

Great Outdoors Inn

Most bed-and-breakfasts in Florida are either Victorian-style or beach-style, with wicker furniture and pastel colours. This is different. Guests check in at the Great Outdoors Trading Company, a shop and café in High Springs. The inn is a sister-business in the country south of town and consists of the innkeepers' house, a swimming-pool and a plain, white, single-storey structure divided into six unusual bedrooms.

The Cat Room is full of felines, with lion faces on the coverlet, prints of a Florida panther and African leopard on the wall and even a leopard-spot shower curtain. The Panda Room has fern wallpaper with a border of pandas and a black carpet. All have handsome beds, made by a local craftsman from heavy, rough, cedar timbers, with orthopaedic foam pads topped by futons. The natural theme works because furnishings are high-quality and rooms are spacious, with high ceilings. Guests seeking further seclusion may follow the trail through the extensive pine woods behind. A breakfast basket brought to the door suits those who prefer a quiet, private start to the day. Others may choose to eat in the Great Outdoors Café in town.

Nearby Ichetucknee Springs State Park, shopping.

c/o The Great Outdoors Trading Co, 65 N Main Street, PO Box 387, High Springs, FL 32643
Tel (904) 454 2900
Fax (904) 454 1225
Location on a country road; ample car parking
Meals breakfast
Prices rooms $$ with breakfast
Rooms 6 double; all have bath or shower, air-conditioning, phone, coffee-maker, microwave oven, refrigerator; TV by request
Facilities garden, swimming-pool, woods
Smoking not permitted
Credit cards MC, V
Children over 12
Disabled 1 adapted room
Closed never
Languages Spanish
Proprietors Tedd Greenwald and Mary Ellen Flowers

Northeast

Bed-and-breakfast, Jacksonville

Cleary-Dickert House

Only a few steps from the St Johns River on the edge of Jacksonville's National Historic District, the unremarkable 80- year old brick and stucco house belongs to a remarkable multilingual couple. Betty Dickert, the epitome of a Southern hostess, steals the spotlight with her wide smile and broad accent. Husband Joe Cleary is British, 'quietly cheerful' and boils the kettle for an authentic afternoon tea.

The hub of the house is the welcoming kitchen, cleverly built into a connecting passage between the main building and The Carriage House. The latter is not only more private, with its own entrance, but also wheelchair accessible. Like the other two bedrooms, colours and fabrics are carefully co-ordinated. Bathrooms are on the small side. Although some may find the overall decoration rather fussy, "it's plain good fun to be here," declared one guest, who relished the low-key atmosphere. 'Spectacular' floral displays and the riot of colour in the garden reflect the green thumb of Betty's mother. Opened in 1994, the large number of repeat guests attests to the inn's popularity with the university, medical and business communities.

Nearby St Johns River, walking, shopping, art galleries.

1804 Copeland Street,
Jacksonville, FL 32204
Tel (904) 387 4762
Location Riverside-Avondale historic district, 10 min from downtown; limited car parking
Meals breakfast
Prices rooms $-$$ with breakfast
Rooms 4 suites; all have bath or shower, air-conditioning, TV
Facilities dining-room, sitting-room; garden
Smoking outdoors only
Credit cards AE, MC, V
Children over 10
Disabled suitable, 1 adapted room
Closed never
Languages French, Greek, Italian, Russian, Spanish
Proprietors Joe Cleary and Betty Dickert

Northeast

Bed-and-breakfast, Jacksonville

House on Cherry Street

Guests who sit on the porch in the late afternoon tend to verge on the poetic as they sip a glass of wine and watch the busy boats on the St Johns River, at the bottom of well-trimmed lawns. Carol Anderson's 1912 house contains a fine collection of antiques, particularly the handsome grandfather clock standing among the delicate Federal and Queen Anne 19thC furniture in the sitting-room. Forget the racks of tourist brochures found in some inns; here, the focus of the entrance hall is a vase of fresh flowers on a central table. Nothing detracts from the overall atmosphere of a gracious private home.

That does not mean it is overly formal. Carol's collection of ducks and decoys adds a touch of whimsy throughout. Each of the four bedrooms has its own sitting-room and we particularly liked the Blue Room, with its antique beds and soothing shades of grey and blue. The Twin Suite with its two beds, foot-to-foot, has fine views. Don't expect whirlpool tubs in the bathrooms: these are old-fashioned but clean and functional.

Carol takes pride in serving 'proper breakfasts'. Streak, the inn dog, is a greyhound with character.

Nearby beaches, shopping, restaurants.

1844 Cherry Street,
Jacksonville, FL 32205
Tel (904) 384 1999
Location on river in Riverside-Avondale district; limited car parking on street
Meals breakfast
Prices rooms $-$$ with breakfast
Rooms 4 suites; all have bath or shower, air-conditioning, TV
Facilities dining-room; porch, garden
Smoking outdoors only
Credit cards MC, V
Children over 10
Disabled not suitable
Closed never
Languages English only
Proprietor Carol Anderson

Northeast

Bed-and-breakfast, Jacksonville

Plantation-Manor Inn

Standing on a quiet block in the National Historic District near the St Johns River, this 1905 mansion could be straight out of *Gone With the Wind.* Owner Jerry Ray is a contractor and his building expertise has been invaluable in renovating the former home of a bank president, with its solid Greek Revival Doric columns and deep wrap-around veranda.

'Grand' by anyone's standards, the decoration is tasteful in the bedrooms without being stuffy. In Crystal, the canopy above the bed balloons up to the ceiling; Polo has an English feel, with a huge roped four-poster bed and a built-in wall television. Country Rose, named after the Laura Ashley fabric, is romantic with an old fireplace. Furnishings in the Louis XVI-style sitting-room, however, verge on the excessive.

The back garden is praised by guests who also use the swimming-pool and hot tub. Jacksonville is not a tourist town, so the bulk of Ray's guests are business people, particularly women travelling on their own. The meeting-room, with its handsome oval walnut dining-table, also has a fax machine. Breakfast, which is 'expanded Continental' is served in the dining-room.

Nearby St Johns River, walking, shopping, galleries.

1630 Copeland Street, Jacksonville, FL 32204
Tel (904) 384 4630
Location Riverside-Avondale Historic District; ample car parking
Meals breakfast
Prices rooms $$-$$$ with breakfast
Rooms 8 double; all have bath or shower, air-conditioning; most have phone, TV
Facilities dining-room, 2 sitting-rooms; veranda, garden, heated outdoor swimming-pool
Smoking outdoors only
Credit cards AE, MC, V
Children over 10
Disabled not suitable
Closed never
Languages English only
Proprietors Jerry and Kathy Ray

Northeast

Bed-and-breakfast, Jacksonville

St Johns House

Joan Moore buys and sells quilts. Her vast sitting-room stretches the entire width of the house and provides a showcase for her ever-changing collection. The kaleidoscope of colour reminded one guest of 'Vasarely's optical puzzles'. Textiles, however, are just one factor in the bold, contemporary decoration ranging from white woodwork on crayon-red walls to bedrooms that are emerald green or vivid blue with intense floral-patterned sheets.

Co-host Dan Schafer is Chair of the History Department at the University of North Florida. His low-key demeanour belies a dry sense of humour that, along with his extensive knowledge of the state, is a bonus for guests who take time to chat. This couple only took up the bed-and-breakfast business in 1993. Joan is a fine chef, creating her own dishes for breakfast such as Scotch eggs, served in the cheery Sun Room. Bathrooms are old-fashioned but large, with stacks of towels.

This 1914-built, 'Prairie-style house'offers something completely different to the dark wood and fussy Victoriana of so many American bed-and-breakfasts. Prices here are particularly attractive but note that credit cards are not accepted.

Nearby walking, jogging; Avondale shopping/dining.

1718 Osceola Street, Jacksonville, FL 32204
Tel (904) 384 3724
Location corner St Johns Ave and Osceola St, Riverside-Avondale Historic District; car parking on street
Meals breakfast
Prices rooms $ with breakfast
Rooms 3 double; 2 with bath or shower, 1 shares bath with hosts; all have air-conditioning
Facilities 2 dining-rooms, sitting-room
Smoking not permitted
Credit cards not accepted
Children very welcome
Disabled not suitable
Closed never
Languages English only
Proprietors Joan Moore, Dan Schafer

Northeast

Historic bed-and-breakfast, Micanopy

Herlong Mansion

Sonny Howard searched all over the USA for the right place to buy for a bed-and-breakfast. As soon as he saw this imposing mansion, he knew that "this is the one." Standing back from the street, the structure dates back to 1845, though the façade was added in 1910, after a particularly lucrative season of raising water melons and pigs. That is local lore; the fact is that the house remained in the Herlong family until 1986.

Inside, the woodwork is exceptional, from the massive staircase to oak floors inlaid with mahogany. We half-expected to see southern belles in crinolines singing at the piano or breakfasting in the dining-room, whose tall windows look into the rather plain garden. Upstairs, a family tree traces the Herlong lineage back to Jacob Herlan, who arrived in the USA in 1735. Brass beds and brick fireplaces, patchwork quilts and carved furniture create the feel of a well-to-do family home. The larger, more expensive rooms are suitably grand but even the smaller John's Room is prettily furnished. With ten bedrooms plus two separate cottages, this is larger than many bed-and-breakfasts. Not surprisingly, it is one of the best-known in the entire state.

Nearby historic houses, antique shops, Gainesville.

Cholokka Boulevard, PO Box 667, Micanopy, FL 32667
Tel and Fax (352) 466 3322; (800) HERLONG
Location in small village; ample car parking
Meals breakfast, afternoon snacks
Prices rooms $-$$$ with breakfast
Rooms 6 double; 4 suites; 2 cottages; all have bath or shower, air-conditioning; 1 Jacuzzi
Facilities dining-room, sitting-room; porches, garden
Smoking outdoors only
Credit cards MC, V
Children welcome
Disabled not suitable
Closed never
Languages English only
Proprietor Sonny Howard

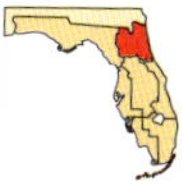

Northeast

Modern bed-and-breakfast, Micanopy

Shady Oak

Micanopy is a 'blink and you'd miss it' village but the name recalls a legendary leader of the Seminoles, the Indian tribe who settled here some 200 years ago. In the last two decades, it has become a popular weekend destination, particularly for collectors of antiques and bric-à-brac. At the main crossroads stands a large building with double-decker wrap-around verandas in the traditional Florida Vernacular style. It looks old but was built in 1988 by Frank James, who moved here because Micanopy is still 'old Florida'. At the front are several shops; behind is Frank's studio for his woodwork and stained glass that feature in the five-room bed-and-breakfast above.

We admired his four-poster bed of southern yellow pine in the master suite, which has its own screened porch, but laughed out loud at the delightful stained glass image of a saucy turn-of-the-century bar girl in Victoria's suite. Although there are some antiques, this is not a place striving to create a Victorian experience. Instead, the feel is stylishly modern and totally relaxing. Breakfast is served in the informal communal area at 9 am or brought on a tray to bedrooms.

Nearby historic houses, shopping, Gainesville.

203 Cholokka Boulevard, PO Box 236, Micanopy, FL 32667
Tel (352) 466 3476
Location in heart of village, above shops; own car parking
Meals breakfast
Prices rooms $$-$$$ with breakfast
Rooms 5 double; all have bath or shower, air-conditioning, TV; some radio, Jacuzzi, CD player
Facilities dining-room/sitting-room; porches, garden
Smoking outdoors only
Credit cards MC, V
Children welcome
Disabled not suitable
Closed never
Languages English only
Managers Candy and Mark Lancaster

Northeast

Resort, Orange Park

The Club Continental

Originally the estate of Caleb Johnson, founder of the Palmolive soap empire, this resort complex is still family-run, now by the fourth generation. First impressions can be confusing, because of the variety of buildings, from private condominiums to The Inn, the original Mira Rio mansion, which is open to overnight guests. Built in 1923, its grandiose, Italianate style includes baronial chandeliers, tapestries and huge carved stone fireplaces. Like film sets, the seven bedrooms are themed as English, French or Mexican. Decorations may not be to everyone's liking, but the 15 bedrooms in the River Suite building are less theatrical, more relaxing and have balconies overlooking the river.

Set in the lushly-landscaped estate are seven tennis courts, two swimming-pools and a marina. At the water's edge is the informal Riverhouse Pub but there is also a restaurant offering more adventurous fare such as salmon on red cabbage with a sherry vinegar glaze. Breakfasts are standard continental. Prices for accommodation vary but all can use the sporting facilities, so active families or groups of friends could have an inexpensive holiday by booking into the modestly-priced rooms.

Nearby Jacksonville (20 min); charter fishing, sailing charters.

2143 Astor Street, PO Box 7059, Orange Park, FL 32073
Tel (904) 264 6070; (800) 877 6070
Fax (904) 264 4044
Location south of Jacksonville, off Rte 17 (Roosevelt Blvd); ample car parking
Meals breakfast, lunch, dinner
Prices rooms $-$$$ with breakfast
Rooms 17 double; 5 suites; all have bath or shower, air-conditioning, phone, TV
Facilities dining-room, 3 sitting-rooms; tennis courts, 2 outdoor swimming-pools
Smoking permitted
Credit cards AE, MC, V
Children very welcome
Disabled suitable, 1 adapted room
Closed never; restaurant only, Sat, Mon, Sun evening
Languages English only
Proprietors Johnson Family

Northeast

Bed-and-breakfast, St Augustine

Carriage Way

St Augustine exploits its title of 'America's oldest European settlement' with the Oldest House, the Oldest Store Museum and even the Authentic Old Jail. It has become a year-round destination, particularly for day trips and romantic weekends. To get the best out of the town, stay overnight and soak up the atmosphere after most of the crowds have gone. Many of the inns have broad verandas where guests can admire the lighted towers of the city and even hear the commentary from the drivers of horse-drawn carriages that regularly clatter past. More authoritative is the owner of the Carriage Way, Bill Johnson, who is a fount of local knowledge as well as a first-rate innkeeper, who turns first-timers into repeat visitors.

Because of the inn's popularity, there have been comments about wear and tear, but these are tempered by praise for Bill, his reasonable prices, and his 'special touches' such as picnics delivered, together with fresh dry towels, to the beach. His best room is the light and bright Elizabeth Gould in the recently-modernized addition at the back. With a four-poster bed under a high cathedral ceiling, it also has a large inviting bathroom.
Nearby historic district, beaches 5 miles (8 km) away.

70 Cuna Street, St Augustine, FL 32084
Tel (904) 829 2467; (800) 908 9832
Fax (904) 826 1461
Location at Cuna St and Cordova St; limited car parking
Meals breakfast, picnics
Prices rooms $-$$ with breakfast
Rooms 9 double; all have bath or shower, air-conditioning, phone, TV
Facilities dining-room, sitting-room; veranda, bicycles
Smoking outdoors only
Credit cards MC, V
Children over 8
Disabled not suitable
Closed never
Languages English only
Proprietors Bill and Diane Johnson

Northeast

Bayside bed-and-breakfast, St Augustine

Casa de la Paz

'Like visiting an aunt who has moved from the Cotswolds to Florida,' decided our inspector after seeing the floral chintz fabrics, the oriental rugs, and European antiques in the 'House of Peace'. Unfortunately, Janet and Jack Maki may be moving, though Janet, who is British, insists that they will only sell to someone who shares their philosophy and high standards.

The Chippendale furniture, crystal, china and sterling silver are a rarity in Florida, as is the proper sit-down breakfast where she serves unusual hot dishes such as scrambled eggs with black-eyed pea relish. All this is a treat for more mature guests who like to get away from bare-foot children in swim-suits and to sample what Americans perceive as European formality.

Jack looks after the abundance of plants in the conservatory and the palm-shaded garden at the back with its display of roses, pansies and impatiens around a trickling fountain. To enjoy his handiwork, stay in the Santa Maria room, which runs the width of the house. Most guests, however, want a bedroom at the front, since this inn is one of only three in St Augustine right on the water, with views of Matanzas Bay.

Nearby historic district, beaches 5 miles (8 km).

22 Avenida Menendez, St Augustine, FL 32084
Tel (904) 829 2915; (800) 929 2915
Location between Treasury St and Hypolita St; limited car parking
Meals breakfast
Prices rooms $-$$$ with breakfast
Rooms 6 double; all have bath or shower, air-conditioning, TV
Facilities 2 dining-rooms, sitting-room; garden
Smoking outdoors only
Credit cards AE, MC, V
Children not suitable
Disabled not suitable
Closed never
Languages English only
Proprietors Janet and Jack Maki

Northeast

Elegant bed-and-breakfast, St Augustine

Casa de Solana

Faye McMurry believes that people remember what they eat more than where they stay, so she takes breakfast seriously. At 8.30 am, guests take their places at the impressive mahogany table which seats eight comfortably. Unlike most hosts, however, Faye does not rush in and out of the kitchen. While uniformed staff serve the two-course meal, she presides, "so that I can listen to visitors' needs and make sure they get the most out of their stay."

Guests remember much more than breakfast, however. Secluded from the rest of the town by high walls, the 18thC Spanish villa is filled with family heirlooms that the McMurrys brought with them from Virginia. Although there are only four suites, each has its own sitting-room, "so you don't see the bed as soon as you walk in," Faye explains, "and there is room to sit and chat, or read." The British suite has views over the bay, while the Minorcan, with old beams, a working fireplace and a large 'marriage tub', opens directly on to the garden.

When the McMurrys opened in 1983, they set a standard that has not been matched by any of the numerous inns which have sprung up since. Luxury at these prices becomes affordable.

Nearby historic district, beaches 5 miles (8 km) away.

21 Aviles Street, St Augustine, FL 32084
Tel (904) 824 3555
Location Aviles St at Cadiz St; own car parking
Meals breakfast
Prices rooms $$$ with breakfast
Rooms 4 suites; all have bath or shower, air-conditioning, TV; 1 with Jacuzzi
Facilities dining-room, sitting-room; garden
Smoking outdoors only
Credit cards AE, MC, V
Children not suitable
Disabled not suitable
Closed never
Languages English only
Proprietor Faye McMurry

Northeast

Bed-and-breakfast, St Augustine

Casa de Sueños

In St Augustine, any inn that has been recently remodelled or redecorated stands out from its competitors. Sandy and Ray Tool have put a lot of effort into their 'House of Dreams'. When they purchased the Spanish-style, turn-of-the-century villa it was being used for offices.

Now it could be a textbook example of an American bed-and-breakfast. They restored architectural features such as the Mediterranean arches and polished the oak floors. They filled the house with the obligatory antiques and lined the dining-room side-board with china and crystal. They reflected the town's Spanish connection by christening their bedrooms with names such as Cordova and Castillo. The former is suitable for special occasions, with a handsome modern Spanish bed and huge Jacuzzi, while the latter is more snug, with its own balcony.

Although this inn only opened in 1995, business visitors have discovered it already thanks to its high-tech conveniences such as e-mail, fax, modem and photocopier. On the other hand, holiday-makers who expect their inns to be relaxed and folksy might find it all just a little too composed.

Nearby historic district, beaches 5 miles (8 km) away.

20 Cordova Street, St Augustine, FL 32084
Tel (904) 824 0887; (800) 824 0804
Fax (904) 825 0074; (800) 735 7534
Location at Cordova St and Saragossa St; limited car parking
Meals breakfast
Prices rooms $$-$$$ with breakfast
Rooms 4 double; 2 suites; all have bath or shower, air-conditioning, phone, TV
Facilities dining-room, sitting-room, fax, copiers, modem; bicycles
Smoking outdoors only
Credit cards MC, V
Children not suitable
Disabled 1 room adapted
Closed never
Languages English only
Proprietors Sandy and Ray Tool

Northeast

Bayside inn, St Augustine

Casablanca Inn

In the Prohibition era of the 1920s, federal law officers made this hotel their base while tracking down importers of illegal liquor. As soon as they left town, legend has it that the owner climbed on to the flat roof to swing a lantern as a signal to the rum-runners that the coast, literally, was clear.

Now, even though the smugglers' boats have been replaced by pleasure boats in Matanzas Bay, the Casablanca Inn remains a visual as well as historic landmark on the waterfront. On the outside, the enormous, Southern-style, squared-off verandas are decorated with balustrades and pillars. Inside, the feeling is of a gracious home, with Vivaldi concertos playing in the background and fine antiques and artwork. More spacious than other inns, the bedrooms are generous, with rejuvenated bathrooms and hammocks hanging on airy porches. Only a gangster's moll, however, would coo over the teddy bears on each bed.

Right outside is the starting point for the horse-drawn carriage tours of the Old City. All this seems to add to the charm for the younger crowd, who choose to stay here rather than at the Casa de la Paz (see p134) just next door.

Nearby historic district, beaches 5 miles (8 km) away.

24 Avenida Menendez, St Augustine, Florida 32084
Tel (904) 829 0928; (800) 826 2626
Fax (904) 826 1892
Location between Hypolita St and Treasury St; ample car parking
Meals breakfast
Prices rooms $$-$$$$ with breakfast
Rooms 12 double; all have bath or shower, air-conditioning; 6 with Jacuzzi
Facilities dining-room, sitting-room; porches, bicycles
Smoking outdoors only
Credit cards AE, MC, V
Children welcome
Disabled 1 adapted room
Closed never
Languages English only
Manager Janet Murray

Northeast

Historic inn, St Augustine

The Kenwood Inn

On a quiet side street in the historic district, the Kenwood Inn was built as an hotel and has been welcoming guests for well over a century. As well as tourists, families visiting nearby Flagler College stay here. The current owners, Mark and Kerrianne Constant are planning to move but are determined that the next owners should continue the combination of comfort and informality that they imposed on the rambling mansion.

The Constants are professional innkeepers, with experience in New Hampshire. Their refreshingly uncomplicated approach aims for relaxation without pretension, allowing the size of the rooms to make the impression, rather than the furnishings. 'Lived-in' is one guest's reaction; 'the slightly faded grandeur of old money ' another. Bathrooms have the eccentricity of old-fashioned plumbing, so may disappoint those who enjoy whirlpool tubs and cascades of hot water. Bedrooms, however, are pleasant and varied, though Scots will be taken aback to find a tartan theme in the Old English room. Number 9 has a private balcony. In a town short on space, the bonus here is the swimming-pool. Even better, the peaceful, walled courtyard is separate.

Nearby historic district, beaches 5 miles (8 km) away.

38 Marine Street, St Augustine, Fl 32084
Tel (904) 824 2116
Fax (904) 824 1689
Location at Marine St and Bridge St; limited on street, public car park nearby
Meals breakfast
Prices rooms $$-$$$ with breakfast
Rooms 10 double; 4 suites; all have bath or shower, air-conditioning
Facilities dining-room, 2 sitting-rooms; veranda, garden, swimming-pool
Smoking outdoors only
Credit cards MC, V
Children over 8
Disabled not suitable
Closed never
Languages English only
Proprietors Mark and Kerrianne Constant

Northeast

Restaurant with rooms, St Augustine

Old City House

In a city that takes its history seriously, most innkeepers hark back to the Victorian or even the Spanish era. The Comptons have taken a different approach. John is a professional chef, so their priority is the restaurant. Instead of lacy curtains and fringed lampshades, the dining-room is coldly contemporary, with track lighting, tile-topped tables and non-descript art. Everything is focused on the imaginative food. Grouper can be baked, with a Dijon mustard, smoked bacon, sour cream and horseradish sauce. Mixed seafood is layered into a *strudel* or tossed in pasta with a lobster sauce.

When this young and enterprising couple took over in 1989, their aim was "to have our own place and do things our way". After renovating the century-old building, the overall result is modern and business-like rather than atmospheric.

Bedrooms are comfortable and fresh-looking but are rather lacking in individuality. The inn is so centrally-located that traffic noise can be intrusive.

Although this is not the place for peaceful naps on a balcony, it is superior to many of the more traditional but rather tired bed-and-breakfasts in town.

Nearby historic district, beaches 5 miles (8 km) away.

115 Cordova Street, St Augustine, FL 32084
Tel (904) 826 0113
Location Cordova St at King St; public car park nearby
Meals breakfast, lunch, dinner
Prices rooms $-$$ with breakfast
Rooms 5 double; all have bath or shower, air-conditioning, TV
Facilities restaurant; patio, bicycles
Smoking outdoors only
Credit cards AE, DC, MC, V
Children welcome
Disabled not suitable
Closed never; restaurant only, Mon
Languages English only
Proprietors Compton family

Northeast

Bed-and-breakfast, St Augustine

The Old Powder House Inn

Manufactured romance is part of the American way of life and Al and Eunice Howes, who came here in 1992, embrace the concept enthusiastically. Their special packages include champagne and strawberries, roses and massage, breakfast in bed and bubble baths. Bedrooms, with names such as Memories and Splendid Time, are on the frilly side of Victoriana. Our inspector felt most comfortable in Grandma's Attic, up on the third floor, where old bonnets and boxes provide decoration, but large windows make it seem airy. Whether Grandma would have approved of joining nine other people in the garden whirlpool tub is open to doubt.

The name of the house has nothing to do with ladies' make-up. It refers to the Spaniards' storehouse of gunpowder which was here until fire destroyed the building around 1800. Nearly a century later, the present house was put up as part of a development of winter vacation homes for well-to-do northerners. Afternoon tea, as well as hors d'oeuvres and wine are included in the prices which are reasonable, though the romantic extras can soon add up. Most bed-and-breakfasts offer only a continental breakfast; here it is a full meal.

Nearby historic district, beaches 5 miles (8 km) away.

38 Cordova Street, St Augustine, FL 32084
Tel (904) 824 4149; (800) 447 4149
Location Between Cuna St and Hypolita St; ample car parking
Meals breakfast, snacks
Prices rooms $-$$ with breakfast
Rooms 9 double; all have bath or shower, air-conditioning; TV by request
Facilities 2 dining-rooms, sitting-room; proches, garden, hot tub
Smoking not permitted
Credit cards MC, V
Children over 10
Disabled not suitable
Closed never
Languages English only
Proprietors Al and Eunice Howes

Northeast

Bed-and-breakfast, St Augustine

Penny Farthing Inn

The penny-farthing bicycle on the front porch is not part of the St Augustine nostalgia trip. Pam and Walt James claim to be the first inn in the Southeastern USA to concentrate on 'bicycling getaways'. Although cycling round the old city is a popular way of seeing the sights, less appreciated are the miles of hard, flat sandy beaches, the inland lanes and the riverside rides along the St Johns. The James have drawn up a dozen detailed route plans ranging from a morning's pedal to a five-day tour.

Not surprisingly, the clientele here is younger than in many other inns, attracted by the exercise, the hearty breakfasts and the sheer unpretentiousness of the owners, who took over the plain, two-storey Victorian house in the summer of 1994. Their decorations are simple but tasteful. We liked the white and blue Brass Room with its brass bed, although the most popular is the Pink Room, with its brass wash-basin, porch and swing.

The inn may be in a rather commercial part of town, away from the narrow streets and clip-clop of horses, but it does have easy parking. This is a bonus, whether you are on a cycling holiday or just taking advantage of the reasonable prices.

Nearby historic district, beaches 5 miles (8 km) away.

83 Cedar Street, St Augustine, FL 32084
Tel (904) 824 2100; (800) 395 1890
Location between US 1 and Granada St; ample car parking
Meals breakfast
Prices rooms $-$$$ with breakfast
Rooms 3 double; 1 suite; all have bath or shower, air-conditioning, TV, private porches, swings
Facilities dining-room, sitting-room; bicycles
Smoking not permitted
Credit cards MC, V
Children over 12
Disabled not suitable
Closed never
Languages English only
Proprietors Pam and Walt James

Northeast

Two-house inn, St Augustine

Southern Wind Inns

First impressions here are unpromising, thanks to overgrown bushes and unkempt trees and grass. Nevertheless, our inspector was pleasantly suprised by the neat, well-kept interior of the turn-of-the-century mansion. Jeanette and Dennis Dean are the down-to-earth couple behind this quirky bed-and-breakfast. For years, satisfied guests signed ceramic tiles which were then applied to the front porch. Now, they cover every possible space, so newcomers can no longer contribute to the collection. They can, however, have the fun of reading them.

Inside, the dining-room is small but inviting, with a well-chosen array of antiques. Bedrooms are more imaginatively-decorated than named: Tapestry is hung with tapestries, while Jacuzzi has a whirlpool tub right in the room.

All this is in Southern Wind East, the main house. Down the street is a separate cottage, with six bedrooms, called Southern Wind West. Designed for families, breakfast is delivered here for those with children though couples are encouraged to walk up to the main inn. Verdict: this is a find, thanks to reasonable rates and unaffected hosts.

Nearby historic district, beaches 5 miles (8 km) away.

18 Cordova Street, St Augustine, FL 32084
Tel (904) 825 3623
Location between Orange St and Saragossa St; public car parking on street
Meals breakfast
Prices rooms $-$$$ with breakfast
Rooms 15 double; all have bath or shower, air-conditioning

Facilities dining-room, sitting-room; porch, garden
Smoking not permitted
Credit cards AE, MC, V
Children welcome
Disabled not suitable
Closed never
Languages English only
Proprietors Jeanette and Dennis Dean

Northeast

Historic bed-and-breakfast, St Augustine

Victorian House

While others rest on their laurels, Daisy Morden and her staff always seem to be busy. During our visit, a room was being repainted, a regular task that other inns in town could imitate more often. Originally from Connecticut, Daisy is an enthusiast who has stencilled the floors and walls of almost all the bedrooms. The Moses Eaton room, named after the famous New England stenciller, has a white tassel pattern on the floor that continues into the bathroom. Jennifer's, by contrast, has cherry floors, white walls, love seats and an antique spool bed, draped with a hand-crocheted canopy. The antique quilt that once lay on the bed is now displayed on a stand.

The popularity of this modest inn is due to more than just the pretty New England look. "There are no rules, guests have the run of the house," says Daisy. They watch TV in the parlour, play cards in the dining-room. In the evening, they relax on the porch or stroll through the old streets.

Unlike some bed-and-breakfasts, a member of staff is always on the premises, even at night. We were impressed by the willingness to provide a proper service at competitive prices, right in the heart of town

Nearby historic district, beaches 5 miles (8 km) away.

11 Cadiz Street, St Augustine, FL 32084
Tel (904) 824 5214
Location Cadiz St at Aviles St; limited car parking
Meals breakfast
Prices rooms $-$$ with breakfast
Rooms 8 double; all have bath or shower, air-conditioning
Facilities dining-room, sitting-room; porches, garden
Smoking outdoors only
Credit cards AE, MC, V
Children over 6
Disabled not suitable
Closed never
Languages English only
Proprietor Daisy Morden

Northeast

Bayside bed-and-breakfast, St Augustine

Westcott House

St Augustine trades on its olde worlde atmosphere, but the charm of narrow cobbled streets and closely-built houses can soon wear thin. What the Westcott House offers is a sense of space. First, there is the large garden, where trees shade a terrace with tables and chairs. Then there are the deep porches, front and back, and, finally, sweeping views across Avenida Menendez to Matanzas Bay, the Bridge of Lions and the yacht pier.

Open for a decade, this claims to be the second oldest bed-and-breakfast in town. Built for Dr Westcott, a notable 19thC local citizen involved in the planning of the Intracoastal Waterway, the house retains the elaborate decoration of the High Victorian era which some find rather fussy. Individual pieces, however, can be eye-catching, such as the sitting-room fireplace with its gold and blue carving and inset mirror. Bedrooms follow the theme, with attractive carved canopy or wrought iron beds.

The professionalism of the owners, plus the uniformed staff, all add up to a rather formal atmosphere for Florida. Thankfully, breakfast is relaxed since guests may choose to eat in their bedrooms, in the garden, or out on the porch.

Nearby historic district, beaches 5 miles (8 km) away.

146 Avenida Menendez, St Augustine, FL 32084
Tel (904) 824 4301
Location Ave Menendez at St Francis; public car parking
Meals breakfast
Prices rooms $$-$$$ with breakfast
Rooms 8 double; all have bath or shower, air-conditioning, phone, TV
Facilities dining-room, sitting-room; porches, garden
Smoking outdoors only
Credit cards MC, V
Children over 8
Disabled not suitable
Closed never
Languages English only
Proprietors David and Sherry Dennison

➠ More on page 177

Greater Miami

Bed-and-breakfast, Coconut Grove

Cherokee Rose Lodge

This elegant 'tropical Tudor' mansion is a gem. In handsome grounds behind a tall coral-rock wall. One suite, sleeping four, is in the main house; the cosy cottage by the swimming-pool sleeps three. Cheryl Guerrero is an enthusiastic hostess.

❖ 3734 Main Highway, Coconut Grove, FL 33133 **Tel** (305) 858 4884 **Fax** (305) 443 3550 **Meals** breakfast **Prices** rooms $$$ with breakfast **Rooms** 2, all with bath or shower, air- conditioning, phone, TV, VCR **Credit cards** not accepted **Children** welcome **Closed** Nov to April **Languages** English, French, German, Italian, Spanish

Art Deco hotel, Miami Beach

Indian Creek Hotel

Just outside the Art Deco District, this busy, friendly hotel is popular with business people who enjoy the slightly more formal atmosphere. Chef Mary Rohan's cooking is a major bonus in the quiet, intimate restaurant. Bedrooms are standard, but well-kept.

❖ 2727 Indian Creek Drive, Miami Beach, FL 33139 **Tel** (305) 531 2727 **Fax** (305) 531 5651 **Meals** breakfast, lunch, dinner **Prices** rooms $$-$$$$ with breakfast **Rooms** 61, all with bath or shower, air-conditioning, phone, TV, radio, minibar **Credit cards** AE, DC, MC, V **Children** very welcome **Closed** never **Languages** English, Spanish

Spanish Colonial hotel, South Miami Beach

Beach Paradise Hotel

New ownership promises to revamp a hotel that had become tired and outdated. The million-dollar renovation has introduced a pale grey colour scheme in bedrooms, with tomato-coloured carpets, pale green bedspreads. Restaurant on ground floor.

❖ 600 Ocean Drive, Miami Beach, FL 33139 **Tel** (305) 531 0021; (800) 258 8886 **Fax** (305) 674 0206 **Meals** breakfast, lunch, dinner **Prices** rooms $$-$$$$ with breakfast **Rooms** 50, all with bath or shower, air-conditioning, phone, TV **Credit cards** AE, DC, MC, V **Children** welcome **Closed** never **Languages** English, French, German

Art Deco hotel, South Miami Beach

Boulevard Hotel

Kamran Koohsari is upgrading this well-known hotel with its bar and outdoor café. Above the usual cramped reception area are identikit bedrooms with cool grey walls, floral bedspreads, blue carpets. Plain, clean, functional bathrooms.

❖ 740 Ocean Drive, Miami Beach, FL 33139 **Tel** (305) 532 0376; **Fax** (305) 674 8179 **Meals** breakfast, lunch, dinner **Prices** rooms $$-$$$$ with breakfast **Rooms** 33, all with bath or shower, air-conditioning, phone, TV **Credit cards** AE, DC, MC, V **Children** welcome **Closed** never **Languages** English, French, German, Italian, Russian, Spanish, Swedish

Greater Miami

Apartment complex, South Miami Beach

Brigham Gardens

Over 100 species of plants flourish in Erika and Hillary Brigham's garden. Quieter, more private than many similarly-priced places, so recommended even though no breakfast is served. Simple but attractive rooms; most have kitchens.

❖ 1411 Collins Avenue, Miami Beach, FL 33139 **Tel** (305) 531 1331 **Fax** (305) 538 9898 **Meals** no meals served **Prices** rooms $-$$$ **Rooms** 18, all with bath or shower, air-conditioning, phone, TV, radio; 12 with kitchen **Credit cards** AE, MC, V **Children** very welcome **Closed** never **Languages** some Spanish

Art Deco hotel, South Miami Beach

The Cavalier

The bedrooms, in exotic purples and oranges, are small; walls are thin and bathrooms tiny. Younger guests who want to be in the heart of the SoBe action are happy here. Breakfast at the Leslie Hotel, next door. Part of the Island Outpost group. Well priced.

❖ 1320 Ocean Drive, Miami Beach, FL 33139 **Tel** (305) 534 2135; (800) OUTPOST **Fax** (305) 531 5543 **Meals** at the Leslie, next door **Prices** rooms $$-$$$$ with breakfast **Rooms** 42, all with bath or shower, air-conditioning, phone, TV, radio, CD, safe **Credit cards** AE, DC, MC, V **Children** welcome **Closed** never **Languages** English, Spanish

Art Deco hotel, South Miami Beach

Colony Hotel

The blue neon Colony sign features in many photos of Ocean Drive by night. Its restaurant spills out on to the pavement. Rooms can be noisy, front or back, but have enough art deco to keep budget travellers happy. Bathrooms are inevitably cramped.

❖ 736 Ocean Drive, Miami Beach FL 33139 **Tel** (305) 673 0088; (800) 2 COLONY **Fax** (305) 532 0762 **Meals** breakfast, lunch, dinner **Prices** rooms $$-$$$$ with breakfast **Rooms** 36, all with bath or shower, air-conditioning, phone, TV **Credit cards** AE, DC, MC, V **Children** welcome **Closed** never; restaurant only, Mon, Tues **Languages** English, German

Modern hotel, South Miami Beach

Deco Walk Hotel

This glass and concrete cube, wedged above a row of shops, contrasts with the surrounding art deco buildings. Italian feel, with square pink and grey bedrooms. Plain bathrooms are more spacious than in older neighbours. Help-yourself breakfast.

❖ 928 Ocean Drive, Miami Beach, FL 33139 **Tel** (305) 531 5511 **Fax** (305) 531 5515 **Meals** breakfast **Prices** rooms $$$ with breakfast **Rooms** 10 double; all with bath or shower, air-conditioning, phone, TV, minibar, hairdrier **Credit cards** AE, DC, MC, V **Children** welcome **Closed** April to Oct **Languages** English, Spanish

Greater Miami

Art Deco hotel, South Miami Beach

The Kent

The largest of the Island Outpost hotels (see Casa Grande p38), this creates a South Beach spirit by using child-like primary colours in the affordable bedrooms. Room 310 is a favourite, since it overlooks the back door of Gianni Versace's mansion.

❖ 1131 Collins Avenue, Miami Beach, FL 33139 **Tel** (305) 531 6771; (800) OUTPOST **Fax** (305) 531 0720 **Meals** at Leslie **Prices** rooms $-$$$ with breakfast **Rooms** 56, all with bath or shower, air-conditioning, phone, TV, radio, minibar, safe **Credit cards** AE, DC, MC, V **Children** very welcome **Closed** never **Languages** English, Spanish

Art Deco hotel, South Miami Beach

The Leslie

The ground floor café/restaurant also hosts guests from the Cavalier and Kent at breakfast. Minimally-furnished small bedrooms resonate with orange walls, purple and turquoise bedclothes. In the heart of the South Beach action.

❖ 1244 Ocean Drive, Miami Beach, FL 33139 **Tel** (305) 534 2135; (800) OUTPOST **Fax** (305) 531 5543 **Meals** breakfast, lunch, dinner **Prices** rooms $$-$$$$ with breakfast **Rooms** 43, all with bath or shower, air-conditioning, phone, TV, radio, CD, safe **Credit cards** AE, DC, MC, V **Children** welcome **Closed** never **Languages** English, Spanish

Bed-and-breakfast suites, South Miami Beach

Lily Guesthouse

The stylish and spacious bedrooms are in two small blocks. Polished wood floors and plain white walls are used as a backdrop for large pieces of solid old furniture and beds. Brightly-tiled bathrooms and streamlined kitchens. Well-priced.

❖ 835 Collins Ave, Miami Beach, FL 33139 **Tel** (305) 535 9900 **Fax** (305) 535 0077 **Meals** breakfast **Prices** rooms $$-$$$$ with breakfast **Rooms** 17 double; all with bath or shower, air-conditioning, phone, TV, kitchenette **Credit cards** AE, DC, MC, V **Children** very welcome **Closed** never **Languages** English, Spanish

Art Deco hotel, South Miami Beach

Waldorf Towers Hotel

Although not as chic as its neighbours, the ground floor restaurant with its old-fashioned paddle fans is always buzzing. The bedrooms, by contrast, are plain in pastel shades with cane furniture. Guests seem happy to pay just to be on Ocean Drive.

❖ 860 Ocean Drive, Miami Beach, FL 33139 **Tel** (305) 531 7684; (800) 933 BEACH **Fax** (305) 672 6836 **Meals** breakfast, lunch, dinner, snacks **Prices** rooms $$-$$$$ with breakfast **Rooms** 45, all with bath or shower, air-conditioning, phone, TV **Credit cards** AE, DC, MC, V **Children** very welcome **Closed** never **Languages** English, Spanish

The Keys

Ocean-side villa, Big Pine Key

Barnacle Bed & Breakfast

A delightful architectural flight of fancy, built round a two-storey atrium. Rooftop deck plus private sunning beach. Two rooms with private entrances. Not far from snorkelling and scuba diving at Looe Key. Tim and Jane Marquis from Louisiana took over in 1995.

❖ Long Beach Rd, Rte 1, PO Box 780A, Big Pine Key, FL 33043 **Tel** (305) 872 3298 **Meals** breakfast **Prices** rooms $$-$$$ with breakfast **Rooms** 4, all with bath or shower, air-conditioning, phone, TV, Jacuzzi **Credit cards** MC, V **Children** over 16 **Closed** never **Languages** English only

Ocean-side villa, Big Pine Key

Casa Grande

Next door to Barnacle (see above) in quiet residential area. Kathleen Threkeld built the hacienda-style house 20 years ago with comfortable rooms. Large screened upstairs deck looks out to sea, down to private beach with shade pavillion, hot tub.

❖ Long Beach Drive, PO Box 430378, Big Pine Key, FL 33043 **Tel** (305) 872 2878 **Meals** breakfast **Prices** rooms $$ with breakfast **Rooms** 3, all with bath or shower, air-conditioning, mini-refrigerator **Credit cards** not accepted **Children** not suitable **Closed** never **Languages** English only

Ocean-side home, Big Pine Key

Deer Run Bed & Breakfast

On the Atlantic coast of Big Pine Key, accommodation in this private home is rather expensive. Large screened porch upstairs above shady terrace. Sue Abbott keeps noisy exotic birds in cages. Key deer wander past along beach. Full breakfast.

❖ Long Beach Drive, PO Box 431, Big Pine Key, FL 33043 **Tel** (305) 872 2015 **Meals** breakfast **Prices** rooms $$ with breakfast **Rooms** 2, both with bath or shower, air-conditioning **Credit cards** not accepted **Children** not suitable **Closed** never **Languages** English only

Ocean-side cottages, Islamorada

The Moorings

Spread throughout an extensive estate right on the Atlantic beach, these 18 up-scale cottages are self-catering only. Ideal for active families, since prices include windsurfers, large swimming-pool, tennis court, boat dock. Two night minimum stay.

❖ 123 Beach Road, Islamorada, FL 33036 **Tel** (305) 664 4708 **Fax** (305) 664 4242 **Meals** no meals served **Prices** cottages $$-$$$ **Cottages** 18, all with bath or shower, air-conditioning, phone, TV, kitchen **Credit cards** MC, V **Children** very welcome **Closed** never **Languages** French

The Keys

Underwater hotel, Key Largo

Jules' Undersea Lodge

Established for over a decade, guests have to scuba dive to enter the world's only underwater hotel, on the bottom of a lagoon. Overnight stays are comfortable, air-conditioned and 'amazing'. Non-certified divers can qualify for the experience in three hours.

❖ 51 Shoreland Drive, Key Largo, FL 33037 **Tel** (305) 451 2353 **Fax** (305) 451 4789 **Meals** breakfast, lunch, dinner **Prices** rooms $$$$ with breakfast **Rooms** 2, all with bath or shower, air-conditioning, phone, TV, radio **Credit cards** AE, DC, MC, V **Children** not suitable **Closed** never **Languages** English only

Garden suites, Key West

Ambrosia House

Completely renovated in 1995, the suites show the flair of David Vass and Paul Vitali. The accent is on quality, from fine linens to the well-landscaped garden. Nude sunbathing allowed by the swimming-pool. No breakfast, several restaurants nearby.

❖ 615 Fleming Street, Key West, FL 33040 **Tel** (305) 296 9838; (800) 535 9838 **Fax** (305) 294 2463 **Meals** no meals served **Prices** rooms $$-$$$ **Rooms** 5, all with bath or shower, air-conditioning, TV, coffee-maker **Credit cards** AE, MC, V **Children** not suitable **Closed** never **Languages** some German

Historic house, Key West

Authors of Key West

In 1992, the Langfitts, and their four cats, took over this popular guest-house on the edge of the Historic District. A small courtyard has a plunge pool; themed rooms have memorabilia of authors with Key West connection. Pleasant, quiet, no surprises.

❖ 725 White Street, Key West, FL 33040 **Tel** (305) 294 7381; (800) 898 6909 **Meals** breakfast **Prices** rooms $-$$$ with breakfast **Rooms** 10, all with bath or shower, air-conditioning, TV, refrigerator **Credit cards** AE, MC, V **Children** not suitable **Closed** never **Languages** English only

Waterside hotel, Key West

Banana Bay Resort and Marina

These modern, well-equipped rooms overlook a small beach on the Gulf. Active types make use of the swimming-pool, beach, fitness equipment and water sports, including dive shop. No history or individual decoration. Just off US 1 before Old Town.

❖ 2319 North Roosevelt Boulevard, Key West, FL 33040 **Tel** (305) 296 6925; (800) BANANA 1 **Fax** (305) 296 2004 **Meals** breakfast, lunch **Prices** rooms $$-$$$$ with breakfast **Rooms** 30, all with bath or shower, air-conditioning, phone, TV, hairdrier, refrigerator **Credit cards** AE, DC, MC, V **Children** over 16 **Closed** never **Languages** some German

The Keys

Historic house complex, Key West

Chelsea House

This complex of four buildings is owned by Gary Williams and Jim Durbin. Rooms vary in size, some with antique, others with modern furnishings. Guests may sunbathe topless by swimming-pool; clothes optional on upper sundeck. 'All welcome' policy.

❖ 707 Truman Avenue, Key West, FL 33040 **Tel** (305) 296 2211; (800) 845 8859 **Fax** (305) 296 4822 **Meals** breakfast **Prices** rooms $$-$$$$ with breakfast **Rooms** 19, all with bath or shower, air-conditioning, phone, TV, radio, hairdrier, refrigerator, safe **Credit cards** AE, MC, V **Children** not suitable **Closed** never **Languages** French, German

Historic bed-and-breakfast, Key West

The Conch House

Despite being in the Holland family since 1889, the look is rather impersonal. Rooms are pretty, with some antiques, but no clutter. This is more of a traditional inn than a 'funky' Key West guest-house. A swimming-pool is wedged into a patio at the back.

❖ 625 Truman Avenue, Key West, FL 33040 **Tel** (305) 293 0020; (800) 207 5806 **Fax** (305) 293 8447 **Meals** breakfast **Prices** rooms $-$$$ with breakfast **Rooms** 6, all with bath or shower, air-conditioning, phone, TV, radio **Credit cards** AE, MC, V **Children** not suitable **Closed** never **Languages** English only

Historic house, Key West

Curry Mansion Inn

Al and Edith Amsterdam's grand landmark house, with its library and billiard-room, is a well-known, thriving business. Be prepared for weddings, conferences and tours by non-residents. The pool-side annexe stays quiet. Guests can use a nearby beach club.

❖ 511 Caroline Street, Key West, FL 33040 **Tel** (305) 294 5349; (800) 253 3466 **Fax** (305) 294 4093 **Meals** breakfast **Prices** rooms $$$-$$$$ with breakfast **Rooms** 28, all with bath or shower, air-conditioning, phone, TV, radio, small refrigerator **Credit cards** AE, MC, V **Children** welcome **Closed** never **Languages** French, German, Spanish

Central inn, Key West

Duval House

One of the larger inns in town, this complex of buildings has a club-like, sociable atmosphere. Breakfast is served by the swimming-pool in the big garden at the back. Bedrooms are simply-decorated rather than special. Own car parking.

❖ 815 Duval Street, Key West, FL 33040 **Tel** (305) 294 1666; (800) 22 DUVAL **Fax** (305) 292 1701 **Meals** breakfast **Prices** rooms $$-$$$$ with breakfast **Rooms** 30, all have bath or shower, air-conditioning, phone **Credit cards** AE, DC, MC, V **Children** over 15 **Closed** never **Languages** English only

The Keys

Modern suites, Key West

Duval Suites

Ed Cox also owns the Pilot House (see p55). Here, the rooms with porches right above noisy Duval Street are popular for October's Fantasy Fest. More peaceful are the cottages behind in the garden with its huge, old avocado tree. Self-catering only.

❖ 724 Duval Street, Key West, FL 33040 **Tel** (305) 294 8719; (800) 648 3780 **Fax** (305) 294 9298 **Meals** no meals served **Prices** rooms $$-$$$$ **Rooms** 8, all with bath or shower, air-conditioning, phone, TV, radio, kitchen **Credit cards** AE, DC, MC, V **Children** welcome **Closed** never **Languages** English only

Historic house, Key West

Eaton Lodge

Three buildings, including one from 1832, were re-opened to guests in 1995 by new owners Carolyn and Stephen West. Elegant, though rooms can be small. All have balcony or porch. Breakfast and cocktails served in large garden. Swimming-pool.

❖ 511 Eaton Street, Key West, FL 33040 **Tel** (305) 292 2170; (800) 294 2170 **Fax** (305) 292 4018 **Meals** breakfast **Prices** $$-$$$$ rooms with breakfast **Rooms** 16, all with bath or shower, air-conditioning, phone, TV, radio; some Jacuzzi, refrigerator **Credit cards** MC, V **Children** not suitable **Closed** never **Languages** English only

Hotel complex, Key West

Eden House

Mike Eden runs a busy, friendly hotel where rooms range from inexpensive 'bed and wash-basin' to pricier suites. The Patio and swimming-pool area is rather cramped. No breakfast is served; guests go to nearby cafés. Quiet is requested after 10 pm.

❖ 1015 Fleming Street, Key West, FL 33040 **Tel** (305) 296 6868; (800) 533 KEYS **Fax** (305) 294 1221 **Meals** none served **Prices** rooms $-$$$$ **Rooms** 42, half with bath or shower; all with air-conditioning; some phone, TV **Credit cards** MC, V **Children** welcome **Closed** never **Languages** some German, Spanish

Bed-and-breakfast, Key West

Frances Street Bottle Inn

Commercial fisherman Bob Elkins' bottle collection decorates the small house which he and his wife, Kady, renovated. Neat, tidy roms, include one adapted for wheelchairs. There is a front and a back patio, but no pool. A 10-min walk from Duval Street.

❖ 535 Frances Street, Key West, FL 33040 **Tel** (305) 294 8530; (800) 294 8530 **Fax** (305) 296 5568 **Meals** breakfast **Prices** rooms $-$$ with breakfast **Rooms** 6, all with bath or shower, air-conditioning **Credit cards** AE, MC, V **Children** welcome **Closed** never **Languages** English only

The Keys

Bed-and-breakfast, Key West

The Mermaid & The Alligator

Innkeepers since 1987, Michael and Ursula Keating have given each room a different look: art deco, Japanese, or Queen Anne. The swimming-pool is in a well-planted garden scented with jasmine. Rooms in the separate Conch House share a bath.

❖ 729 Truman Avenue, Key West, FL 33040 **Tel** (305) 294 1894 **Meals** breakfast **Prices** rooms $-$$$ with breakfast **Rooms** most with bath or shower; all with air-conditioning **Credit cards** AE, MC, V **Children** not suitable **Closed** never **Languages** German, some French, Spanish

Historic inn, Key West

The Palms Hotel

Families are welcome at David Taylor's house, where the big swimming-pool is the main attraction. Built in 1889, the upstairs porch looks straight into palm tree fronds but there are modern poolside rooms as well. At the eastern end of the Old Town.

❖ 820 White Street, Key West, FL 33040 **Tel** (305) 294 3146; (800) 558 9374 **Fax** (305) 294 8463 **Meals** breakfast **Prices** rooms $$-$$$$ with breakfast **Rooms** 25, all with bath or shower, air-conditioning, phone, TV, radio **Credit cards** AE, MC, V **Children** very welcome **Closed** never **Languages** Spanish

Cottage bed-and-breakfast, Key West

Papa's Hideaway

'Papa' is Ernest Hemingway, who lived in Key West. His novels are in the simple rooms with slatted doors, wicker furniture. Pat McGee and Ellen Nowlin have a small garden with a plunge pool. By the US naval station but on back lane, this is truly quiet.

❖ 309 Louisa Street, Key West, FL 33040 **Tel** (305) 294 7709; **Fax** (305) 296 1354; (800) 714 7709 **Meals** breakfast **Prices** rooms $$-$$$$ with breakfast **Rooms** 6, all with bath or shower, air-conditioning, phone, TV, kitchenette **Credit cards** MC, V **Children** welcome **Closed** never **Languages** English only

Historic bed-and-breakfast, Key West

La Pensione

In 1891, the Lightbourn cigar-making family built this large, gracious home, wrapped in two-tiers of verandas. The restrained decoration and quiet ambience are relaxing, while Carl Porter is a thoughtful, welcoming manager. Swimming-pool, car parking.

❖ 809 Truman Avenue, Key West, FL 33040 **Tel** (305) 292 9923 **Fax** (305) 296 6509 **Meals** breakfast **Prices** rooms $-$$$ with breakfast **Rooms** 7, all with bath or shower, air-conditioning, phone **Credit cards** AE, MC, V **Children** not suitable **Closed** never **Languages** English only

The Keys

Bed-and-Breakfast complex, Key West

Westwinds

The main house faces one of the larger streets in the Old Town, but there are four small cottages behind in the garden. Rooms are simply-furnished with wicker and cane. Pleasant, if unexciting, the style is low-key and casual. Swimming-pool.

❖ 914 Eaton Street, Key West, FL 33040 **Tel** (305) 296 4440; (800) 788 4150 **Fax** (305) 293 0931 **Meals** breakfast **Prices** rooms **$- $$$** with breakfast **Rooms** 22, 2 share bath or shower; all with air-conditioning, phone **Credit cards** AE, MC, V **Children** over 12 **Closed** never **Languages** German

Bed-and-breakfast, Key West

White Street Inn

George Pentz is also a co-owner of the Paradise Inn (see p54). Here, he and Carla Biscardi converted three houses, opened up the small back gardens and put in a brick patio and swimming-pool. No surprises, informal. At eastern end of Old Town.

❖ 905-907 White Street, Key West, FL 33040 **Tel** (305) 295 9599; (800) 207 9767 **Fax** (305) 295 9503 **Meals** breakfast **Prices** rooms $-$$$ with breakfast **Rooms** 8, all with bath or shower, air-conditioning, phone, TV **Credit cards** AE, DC, MC, V **Children** welcome **Closed** never **Languages** German; some French, Italian

Family bed-and-breakfast, Key West

Wicker Guesthouse

Mark and Libby Curtis, who have three boys, welcome children to their 6-building inn, with its playhouse and swimming-pool in the large garden. Two communal kitchens are a boon for parents. Plain, simple and fresh-looking; some rooms share bathrooms.

❖ 913 Duval Street, Key West, FL 33040 **Tel** (305) 296 4275; (800) 880 4275 **Meals** breakfast **Prices** rooms $-$$$ with breakfast **Rooms** 19, some share bath; all with air-conditioning; some TV, kitchenette **Credit cards** AE, MC, V **Children** very welcome **Closed** never **Languages** English only

Restored house, Key West

William Anthony House

Tony Minore and Bill Beck won awards for restoring this small 1900-built house. One room is adapted for wheelchair users. A social place, where guests gather for afternoon drinks, this is an 'all welcome' inn, but the gay flavour may not suit everyone.

❖ 613 Caroline Street, Key West, FL 33040 **Tel** (305) 294 2887; (800) 613 CAROLINE **Fax** (305) 294 9209 **Meals** breakfast, cocktails **Prices** rooms $$-$$$$ with breakfast **Rooms** 6, all with bath or shower, air-conditioning, TV, radio, refrigerator **Credit cards** AE, MC, V **Children** not suitable **Closed** never **Languages** English only

The Keys

Island cottage complex, Marathon

Conch Key Cottages

Follow the little causeway from US 1 to this private hideaway where guests snorkel from the dock, laze on the beach and swim in the pool. Wayne Burnes and Ron Wilson landscaped the gardens, redecorated and up-graded the self-catering cottages.

❖ Little Conch Key, Rt 1. PO Box 424, Marathon,FL 33050 **Tel** (305) 289 1377; (800) 330 1577 **Meals** no meals served **Prices** rooms $-$$$$ **Cottages** 9, all with bath or shower, air-conditioning, TV, radio, kitchen **Credit cards** MC, V **Children** over 8 **Closed** never **Languages** English only

Bed-and-breakfast, Plantation Key

Casa Thorn

Thorn Trainer's home, on a quiet residential street off US 1, is densely-packed with unusual treasures from all over the world. Some rooms are a little cramped; the small garden behind has orchids and a plunge pool. Private beach just a short walk away.

❖ 114 Palm Lane, MM 87.5 on US 1, Plantation Key, FL 33040 **Tel** (305) 852 3996 **Meals** breakfast **Prices** rooms $-$$$$ with breakfast **Rooms** 5, all with bath or shower, air-conditioning, phone, TV, radio; most with small refrigerator **Credit cards** not accepted **Children** not suitable **Closed** never **Languages** English only

Other recommendations

❖ **Key West:** Tropical Inn, 812 Duval Street, Key West, FL 33040. Tel: (305) 294 9977. $-$$$. 5 rooms. Converted 19thC house in the heart of the Old Town but with a quiet, sedate ambience. Conventional furnishings of wicker and rattan.

❖ **Key West**: Whispers, 409 William Street, Key West, FL 33040. Tel (305) 294 5969; (800) 856 SHHH. $-$$$. 8 rooms. Enthusiastic hosts are making an effort, though the house is rather cluttered. Some shared bathrooms. No swimming-pool.

Key West

Gay and lesbian inns

Although Key West has dozens of hotels, inns and bed-and-breakfasts, some are exclusively for the gay and/or lesbian vacationer. We have listed a selection of the best of these in the historic Old Town.

Alexander's Guesthouse

Owner Michael Ingram is an architect and his stylish taste is obvious throughout this elegant 1910 house which is still his home. Small swimming-pool; a short stroll from Duval Street.

❖ 1118 Fleming Street, Key West, FL 33040 **Tel** (305) 294 9919; (800) 654 9919 **Fax** (305) 295 0357 **Meals** breakfast **Prices** rooms $$-$$$$ with breakfast **Rooms** 15, all with bath or shower, air-conditioning, phone, TV **Credit cards** AE, MC, V **Closed** never

Big Ruby's Guesthouse

In the heart of the Old Town, three houses with dense gardens are hidden behind a high fence. A full, hot breakfast is served poolside. Primarily male clientele, but gay women are welcome.

❖ 409 Appelrouth Lane, Key West, FL 33040 **Tel** (305) 296 2323; (800) 477 7829 **Fax** (305) 296 0281 **Meals** breakfast **Prices** rooms $-$$$$ with breakfast **Rooms** 17, all with bath or shower, air-conditioning, TV **Credit cards** AE, MC, V **Closed** never

The Brass Key Guesthouse

Coming from the Ritz-Carlton organization, Michael MacIntyre's professional background shows in this top-of-the-market guesthouse. Opened in 1986, it still sets the standard.

❖ 412 Frances Street, Key West, FL 33040 **Tel** (305) 296 4719; (800) 932 9119 **Fax** (305) 296 1994 **Meals** breakfast **Prices** rooms $-$$$$ with breakfast **Rooms** 16, all with bath or shower, air-conditioning, phone, TV **Credit cards** AE, MC, V **Closed** never

Colours: The Guest Mansion

Michael Barron's popular Key West inn is in a former cigar factory owner's Victorian mansion, complete with pool and lush garden. Colours has branches in Miami and Costa Rica.

❖ 410 Fleming Street, Key West, FL 33040 **Tel** (305) 294 6977; (800) ARRIVAL **Fax** (305) 534 0362 **Meals** breakfast **Prices** rooms $$-$$$$ with breakfast **Rooms** 12, all with bath or shower, air-conditioning, phone, TV **Credit cards** AE, MC, V **Closed** never

Coral Tree Inn

Water sports are Graeme Smith's selling points here, and across the street at the Oasis, which he also runs. As well as two pools, there is a Jacuzzi big enough for twenty-four. Both inns all male.

❖ 822 Fleming Street, Key West, FL 33040 **Tel** (305) 296 2131; (800) 362 7477 **Meals** breakfast **Prices** rooms $$-$$$$ with breakfast **Rooms** 11, all with bath or shower, air-conditioning, phone, TV **Credit cards** AE, DC, MC, V **Closed** never

Key West

Curry House

Not to be confused with the Curry Mansion. This well-managed men-only inn attracts European as well as American guests. All bedrooms open on to a deck or porch; two share a bathroom.

❖ 806 Fleming Street, Key West, FL 33040 **Tel** (305) 294 6777; (800) 633 7439 **Fax** (305) 294 5332 **Meals** breakfast **Prices** rooms $$-$$$ with breakfast **Rooms** most have bath or shower, air-conditioning, radio, refrigerator **Credit cards** AE, MC, V **Closed** never

La Terraza

A high-profile, social place, with a noisy bar and restaurant, this hotel is known as La Te Da. Open to all, though the image remains gay, with drag shows and a legendary Sunday tea dance.

❖ 1125 Duval Street, Key West, FL 33040 **Tel** (305) 296 6706; (800) LA TE DA-O **Meals** breakfast, lunch, dinner **Prices** rooms $-$$$$ with breakfast **Rooms** 16, all with bath or shower, air-conditioning, phone, TV **Credit cards** AE, MC, V **Closed** never

Mangrove House

This small, well-priced, exclusively male inn has only five bedrooms but is known for its splendid, large, solar-heated pool. The French owner lives on the premises. Two blocks from Duval.

❖ 623 Southard Street, Key West, FL 33040 **Tel** (305) 294 1866; (800) 294 1866 **Fax** (305) 294 8757 **Meals** breakfast **Prices** rooms $-$$$ with breakfast **Rooms** 5, all with bath or shower, air-conditioning, phone, TV **Credit cards** AE, MC, V **Closed** never

The Pines Guesthouse

Off southern Duval Street, the Atlantic Ocean is minutes away but there is also a large swimming-pool. Popular for 20 years, most guests are male, but lesbian couples are also welcome.

❖ 521 United Street, Key West, FL 33040 **Tel** (305) 296 7467; (800) 282 PINE **Fax** (305) 296 3928 **Meals** breakfast **Prices** rooms $-$$$ with breakfast **Rooms** 9, all with bath or shower, air-conditioning, phone, TV, **Credit cards** AE, DC, MC, V **Closed** never

Rainbow House

This is the only Key West inn specifically for women. Neat and tidy, with low-key furnishings, it is only two blocks from the beach. A concierge can book cruises, snorkelling and massages.

❖ 525 United Street, Key West, FL 33040 **Tel** (305) 292 1450; (800) 74 WOMYN **Fax** (305) 293 9829 **Meals** breakfast **Prices** rooms $-$$$$ with breakfast **Rooms** 7, all with bath or shower, air-conditioning, phone, TV **Credit cards** AE, MC, V **Closed** never

Sea Isle Resort

Converted from a motel, this is a clean and unpretentious place to stay, with plain furnishings. The swimming-pool and fully equipped gymnasium are a big draw, as are the reasonable prices.

❖ 915 Windsor Lane, Key West, FL 33040 **Tel** (305) 294 5188; (800) 995 4786 **Fax** (305) 296 7143 **Meals** breakfast **Prices** rooms $$-$$$ **Rooms** 24 , all with shower, air-conditioning, phone, TV
Credit cards MC, V Closed never

Southwest

Island hotel, Cabbage Key

Cabbage Key

Accessible only by boat, this is genuine Old Florida, once day-trippers have gone home. Bedrooms and cottages are plain, with old-fashioned plumbing. The famous bar-restaurant, papered with autographed dollar bills, has surprisingly trendy food.

❖ PO Box 200, Pineland, FL 33945 **Tel** (941) 283 2278 **Fax** (941) 283 1384 **Meals** breakfast, lunch, dinner **Prices** rooms $-$$$$ with breakfast **Rooms** 12, all with bath or shower, air-conditioning **Credit cards** MC, V **Children** welcome **Closed** never **Languages** English

Canoe camp, Everglades City

The Ivey House

Adventurous types wanting to explore the Everglades should book in here. David Harraden runs canoe, nature and camping trips, using the 75-year old house as a base. Rooms are simple but clean; guests share separate men's and women's bathrooms.

❖ 107 Camellia Street, Everglades City, FL 33929 **Tel** (941) 695 3299 **Fax** (941) 695 4155 **Meals** breakfast, dinner **Prices** rooms $ with breakfast **Rooms** 10, all with air-conditioning; shared bathrooms **Credit cards** MC, V **Children** very welcome **Closed** May to Oct **Languages** English only

Riverside hotel, Everglades City

Rod and Gun Lodge

Like the Ivey House (above), this is useful for exploring the Everglades, though simple bedrooms are in old-fashioned motel-like units. Restaurant, bar, swimming-pool at the historic lodge. Rather brash. Walt Disney movie *Gone Fishing* filmed here.

❖ PO Box 190, Everglades City, FL 33929 **Tel** (813) 695 2101 **Meals** breakfast, lunch, dinner **Prices** rooms $-$$, charge for breakfast **Rooms** 17, all with bath or shower, air-conditioning, phone, TV **Credit cards** not accepted **Children** very welcome **Closed** never **Languages** English only

Beach bed-and-breakfast, Fort Myers at Sanibel

Seaside Inn

If the Song of the Sea (see p59) is full, its sister inn is a fine alternative for those wanting to be right on the famous sea-shell strewn sands. Complete renovation in 1995 added character to this complex around a swimming-pool. Bicycles available.

❖ 541 East Gulf Drive, Sanibel, FL 33957 **Tel** (941) 472 1400; (800) 831 7384; in Europe (44 181) 367 5175 **Fax** (941) 481 4947; in Europe (44 181) 367 9949 **Meals** breakfast **Prices** rooms $$$-$$$$ with breakfast **Rooms** 32, all with bath or shower, air-conditioning, phone, TV **Credit cards** AE, DC, MC, V **Children** very welcome **Closed** never **Languages** English only

Southwest

Seaside villa, Ft Myers Beach

The Beach House

Ft Myers Beach is lined with condominiums, but these are self-catering apartments. Audrey Harris and her family welcome other families who enjoy being right on the beach, with play-house and barbecue. Expect basic, plain rooms at budget-prices.

❖ 44960 Estero Boulevard, Ft Myers Beach, FL 33931 **Tel** (941) 463 4004; (800) 226 4005 **Meals** no meals served **Prices** rooms $-$$$ **Rooms** 12, all with bath or shower, air-conditioning, phone, TV, kitchen **Credit cards** MC, V **Children** very welcome **Closed** never **Languages** English only

Gulfshore bed-and-breakfast, Naples

Inn by the Sea

Peggy Cormer's New England-style home, with its patchwork quilts and stencilling, is our only recommendation in this affluent, popular, seaside town, whose heart feels like a small village. The famous fishing pier and upmarket shops are only minutes away.

❖ 287 Eleventh Avenue South, Naples, FL 333940 **Tel** (941) 649 4124; (800) 584 1268 **Meals** breakfast **Prices** rooms $$ with breakfast **Rooms** 5, all with bath or shower, air-conditioning **Credit cards** MC, V **Children** over 14 **Closed** never **Languages** English only

Island resort, North Captiva Island

North Captiva Island Club

Part resort, part wildlife refuge, the island is accessible only by boat or private plane. Ideal for sporty types, with tennis courts, restaurants, swimming-pool. Three-night minimum stay in luxury home or condominium. Fishing and boat charters available.

❖ PO Box 1000, Pineland. FL 33945 **Tel** (813) 395 1001; (800) 576 7343 **Fax** (813) 472 5836 **Meals** breakfast, lunch, dinner **Prices** rooms $$-$$$$ **Rooms** 50, all with bath or shower, air-conditioning, phone, TV **Credit cards** AE, DC, MC, V **Children** very welcome **Closed** never **Languages** English only

Southeast

Waterside apartments, Ft Lauderdale

Banyan Marina

In the land of apartments, these are the exception, with only 10 sophisticated suites, set in gardens overlooking the Intracoastal Waterway. On an island across from Las Olas Boulevard, they are an affordable luxury. Minimum week-long bookings. Docks.

❖ 111 Isle of Venice, Ft Lauderdale, FL 33301 **Tel** (305) 524 4430 **Fax** (305) 764 4870 **Meals** none **Prices** rooms $$$$ per week **Rooms** 10, all with bath or shower, air-conditioning, phone, TV, radio, kitchen **Credit cards** MC, V **Children** welcome **Closed** never **Languages** German

Bed-and-breakfast, Palm Beach

Palm Beach Historic Inn

The Spanish-Colonial exterior promises more than the lacy Victorian interiors deliver. Ideally sited one block from the sea, two blocks from Worth Avenue. A cramped spot to stay, but among the millionaires, Melissa Laitman's prices are affordable.

❖ 365 South County Road, Palm Beach, FL 33480 **Tel** (407) 832 4009 **Fax** (407) 832 6255 **Meals** breakfast **Prices** rooms $$-$$$$ with breakfast **Rooms** 13, all with bath or shower, air-conditioning, phone, TV **Credit cards** AE, MC, V **Children** over 12 **Closed** never **Languages** English only

Condominiums, Pembroke Pines

Raintree Golf Resort

The luxury suites, with every convenience, are right on the nine-year old, par 72 championship course. Golf packages include accommodation, breakfast, 18 holes and a cart. Modern club-house, restaurant. 20 min west of Ft Lauderdale beach.

❖ 1600 South Hiatus Road, Pembroke Pines, FL 33025 **Tel** (305) 432 1500; (800) 346 5332 **Fax** (305) 436 7958 **Meals** breakfast, lunch, dinner **Prices** rooms $$-$$$$ with breakfast **Rooms** 24, all with bath or shower, air-conditioning, phone, TV, kitchen **Credit cards** AE, MC, V **Children** welcome **Closed** never **Languages** English only

Private guest-house, West Palm Beach

West Palm Beach Bed & Breakfast

Dennis Keimel's compact home is in the Old Northwood Historic District, but feels relaxed, like a beach cottage. White wicker furniture, bold tropical colours and swimming-pool in the back yard make this an affordable base in an up-market area.

❖ 419 32nd Street, West Palm Beach, FL 33407 **Tel** (407) 848 4064; (800) 736 4064 **Fax** (407) 842 1688 **Meals** breakfast **Prices** rooms $-$$ with breakfast **Rooms** 4, all with bath or shower, air-conditioning, phone, TV **Credit cards** AE, DC, MC, V **Children** not suitable **Closed** never **Languages** English only

Central West

Water-side home, Apollo Beach

Apollo Beach Bed & Breakfast

Josef and Dorothy Molnar live right on the water, so guests fish from the dock and rent their catamaran to sail in the bay. The colourful windows in their Spanish-style home are a tribute to Mrs Molnar's skill with stained glass; her studio is on site here.

❖ 6350 Cocoa Lane, Apollo Beach, FL 33572 **Tel** (813) 645 2471 **Meals** breakfast **Prices** rooms $ with breakfast **Rooms** 4, all with bath or shower, air-conditioning **Credit cards** not accepted **Children** welcome **Closed** never **Languages** Hungarian

Gulfshore inn, Bradenton, at Bradenton Beach

Duncan House

This pink-and-purple 1910 house, with its simple Victorian-style rooms, is just across the road from the beach in the more commercial part of Anna Maria Island. Becky and Joe Garbus have added a swimming-pool and renovated a second house.

❖ 1703 Gulf Drive, Bradenton Beach, FL 34217 **Tel** (941) 778 6858 **Meals** breakfast **Prices** rooms $-$$ with breakfast **Rooms** 7 rooms, all with bath or shower, air-conditioning **Credit cards** AE, MC, V **Children** welcome **Closed** never **Languages** English only

Gulfshore rooms, Bradenton, at Bradenton Beach

Queen's Gate

Londoner Michael Northfield upgraded this low, modern building across the road from the beach in 1994. Now, white balustrades, a gazebo, and individual furnishings add character. No breakfast served, but there is an extra-large swimming-pool.

❖ 1101 Gulf Drive, Bradenton Beach, FL 34217 **Tel** (941) 778 7153; (800) 310 7153; in UK (0800) 966 097 **Meals** no meals served **Prices** rooms $-$$ **Rooms** 12, all with bath or shower, air-conditioning, phone, TV, refrigerator, coffee-maker **Credit cards** AE, MC, V **Children** very welcome **Closed** never **Languages** English only

Gulfside villa, Bradenton, at Holmes Beach

Alamanda Villa

Right on the superb beach of Anna Maria Island, this large villa was bought by Canadians Greg and Truusje Mitchell in 1994. They redecorated, upgraded kitchens and put new bathrooms into these self-catering apartments. Excellent value for money.

❖ 102 39th Street, Holmes Beach, FL 34217 **Tel** (941) 778 4170 **Meals** no meals served **Prices** rooms $-$$ with breakfast **Apartments** 8, all with bath or shower, air-conditioning, TV, kitchen **Credit cards** not accepted **Children** very welcome **Closed** never **Languages** Dutch, French, German

Central West

Gulfside inn, Bradenton, at Holmes Beach

The Beach Inn

Stephen Hogan offers more than many other inns on the Gulf. He sets out a varied breakfast, arranges room service from the Bistro restaurant next door, and can also organize sessions at the world-famous Nick Bollettieri Tennis Center only 15 min away.

❖ 101 66th Street, Holmes Beach, FL 34217 **Tel** (941) 778 9597; (800) 823 2247 **Fax** (941) 778 8303 **Meals** breakfast **Prices** rooms $-$$ with breakfast **Rooms** 14, all with bath or shower, air-conditioning, phone, TV, hairdrier, mini-refrigerator **Credit cards** MC, V **Children** very welcome **Closed** never **Languages** English only

Stud farm bed-and-breakfast, Brooksville

L&M Paso Fino Ranch

Away from it all in rolling hills, Lowell and Melinda Ensinger breed and train paso fino horses for showing. Guests can hike, admire the horses and use the swimming-pool, though the tennis court is a little overgrown. Simple, clean ranch accommodation.

❖ 5114 Spring Lake Highway, Brooksville, FL 34601 **Tel** (352) 544 0299 **Meals** breakfast, snacks **Prices** rooms $ with breakfast **Rooms** 6, 2 with bath or shower; all with air-conditioning **Credit cards** not accepted **Children** very welcome **Closed** never **Languages** English only

Town bed-and-breakfast, Dade City

Azalea House

Dade City typifies the small, old-fashioned towns that many vacationers never see. Floridians who come here for the antiques shops stay in Grace Bryant's pink-and-white, turn-of-the-century house. Opened in 1995, this is homey, comfortable and pretty.

❖ 37719 Meridian Avenue, Dade City, FL 33525 **Tel** (352) 523 1773 **Meals** breakfast, snacks **Prices** rooms $$ with breakfast **Rooms** 2, all with bath or shower, air-conditioning, TV **Credit cards** AE, MC, V **Children** over 5 **Closed** never **Languages** English only

Riverside units, Homosassa

The Last Resort

The beautiful unspoiled Homosassa River is famous for its wildlife, so it attracts fishermen, boaters and nature lovers. These modern, modular units really are right on the river, standing on stilts. Self-catering only, but Woody's restaurant is 5 min away.

❖ 10738 Halls River Road, Homosassa, FL 34448 **Tel** (352) 628 7117 **Meals** none served **Prices** rooms $$ **Rooms** 6, all with bath or shower, air-conditioning, phone, TV **Credit cards** MC, V **Children** very welcome **Closed** never **Languages** English only

Central West

Riverside bed-and-breakfast, Palmetto

Five Oaks Inn

Rita Tyson is the only innkeeper we have met who is licensed to perform weddings. The early 1900s house overlooking the Manatee River has antiques and fine woodwork, but carpets and curtains need upgrading. Bradenton is just across the bridge.

❖ 1102 Riverside Drive, Palmetto, FL 34221 **Tel** (941) 723 1236 **Meals** breakfast **Prices** rooms $-$$ with breakfast **Rooms** 4, all with bath or shower, air-conditioning, phone **Credit cards** AE, MC, V **Children** not suitable **Closed** never **Languages** English only

Bed-and-breakfast, Plant City

Rysdon House

Best known for its strawberry production, this example of 'small town America' is handy for both Tampa and Orlando. Rick and Claudia Rysdon's 85-year old house is decorated in Victorian style, with a wrap-around porch. Swimming-pool and hot tub.

❖ 702 West Reynolds Street, Plant City, FL 33566 **Tel** (941) 752 8717 **Meals** breakfast, snacks **Prices** rooms $-$$ with breakfast **Rooms** 4, all with bath or shower, air-conditioning, TV, refrigerators **Credit cards** AE, MC, V **Children** welcome **Closed** never **Languages** English only

Waterside bed-and-breakfast, Ruskin

Ruskin House

Professor of literature Dr Miller hosts guests in his spacious house on an inlet of Tampa Bay, near a small beach, marina and wildlife parks. Although filled with antiques, this makes an informal, well-priced base for Tampa, St Petersburg, Sarasota.

❖ 120 Dickman Drive SW, Ruskin, FL 33570 **Tel** (813) 645 3842 **Meals** breakfast **Prices** rooms $ with breakfast **Rooms** 3, 2 with bath or shower; all with air-conditioning **Credit cards** not accepted **Children** over 6 **Closed** never **Languages** English only

Beach villa, St Petersburg at Indian Rocks Beach

The Granger House

Although the driveway runs off a main road, Beverly Granger's 1901-built house is quiet and right on the sand. Balconies and decks provide maximum enjoyment of the Gulfside setting. The deluxe suite could sleep eight. Remarkable value for money.

❖ 610 Gulf Boulevard, Indian Rocks Beach, FL 34635 **Tel** (813) 593 5518 **Fax** (813) 593 1698 **Meals** no meals served **Prices** rooms $ **Rooms** 4, all with bath or shower, air-conditioning, phone, TV, kitchen **Credit cards** MC, V **Children** very welcome **Closed** never **Languages** English only

Central West

Beach villas, St Petersburg at Indian Shores

Endless Summer

One two-storey building is right on the sand, the other is just behind. Colvin and Maryanne Rouse's six comfortable, well-priced apartments are rented by the week. Canadians and Europeans come to this this quiet, mainly residential community.

❖ 19804 Gulf Boulevard, Indian Shores, FL 34635 **Tel** (813) 593 1182 **Fax** (813) 254 5070 **Meals** no meals served **Prices** apartments $-$$$ **Rooms** 6, all with bath or shower, air-conditioning, phone, TV, kitchen **Credit cards** not accepted **Children** very welcome **Closed** never **Languages** English only

Luxury house, St Petersburg at Treasure Island

DaSilva's Designer Suites

An unexpected gem hidden among villas off the busy main road. Three plush self-catering suites, with swimming-pool, were opened in 1995 by the DaSilva family, who have a decorating/building company. Less than one minute from the beach.

❖ 11921 Sunshine Lane, Treasure Island, FL 33706 **Tel** (813) 895 0045; (800) 284 4575 **Fax** (813) 821 0847 **Meals** no meals served **Prices** rooms $$-$$$ **Rooms** 3, all with bath or shower, air-conditioning, phone, TV, VCR, kitchens **Credit cards** not accepted **Children** not suitable **Closed** never **Languages** English only

Gulfshore complex, St Petersburg Beach

Inn on the Beach

The historic district of Pass-A-Grille is the most attractive part of Petersburg Beach. Just across the street from the sand, this small modern complex has been renovated, with pleasant furnishings. Woody Miller is the bluff, hearty manager.

❖ 1401 Gulf Way, St Petersburg Beach, FL 33706 **Tel** (813) 360 8844 **Meals** breakfast on Sat, Sun **Prices** rooms $-$$ **Rooms** 12, all with bath or shower, air-conditioning, phone, TV, kitchen **Credit cards** AE, DC, MC, V **Children** very welcome **Closed** never **Languages** English only

Gulfshore apartments, St Petersburg Beach

Sabal Palms

Also in Pass-A-Grille and across the street from the sand. Joe Caruso runs the complex of simple, plain, self-catering apartments in a renovated 1926 building. Useful for budget-minded beach lovers, with restaurants, shops a stroll away.

❖ 1301 Gulf Way, St Petersburg Beach, FL 33706 **Tel** (813) 367 1305; (800) 770 GULF **Fax** (813) 360 2313 **Meals** no meals served **Prices** rooms $-$$ **Rooms** 10, all with bath or shower, air-conditioning, phone, TV, kitchen **Credit cards** MC, V **Children** very welcome **Closed** never **Languages** English only

Central West

Waterside complex, St Petersburg Beach

Scorpio Bayside

At the northern end of the island, the low building is on Boca Ciega Bay, not the beach. Overhauled in 1991 by the Atkins family from England, the self-catering suites are simple but well-priced, with a swimming-pool and dock. Restaurants are nearby.

❖ 8701 Boca Ciega Drive, St Petersburg Beach, FL 33706 **Tel** (813) 367 5035 **Meals** no meals served **Prices** rooms $-$$ **Rooms** 7, all with bath or shower, air-conditioning, TV, kitchen **Credit cards** MC, V **Children** very welcome **Closed** never **Languages** English only

Rural bed-and-breakfast, Sarasota

Mossy Oak Farm

Deborah and Darrell Williams offer homey comforts and a full breakfast in their rustic-looking farmhouse which is well inland and set among fruit farms. Porches front and back overlook grazing sheep and goats. Guests can fish and canoe on the pond.

❖ 651 Myakka Road, Sarasota, FL 34240 **Tel** (941) 322 0604 **Meals** breakfast, picnic lunches, snacks **Prices** rooms $$ with breakfast **Rooms** 3, all with bath or shower, air-conditioning, phone, TV **Credit cards** not accepted **Children** not suitable **Closed** never **Languages** English only

Island suites, Sarasota at Lido Key

Lido Beach Palms

One block from the beach, these low, yellow-and-white buildings enclose a swimming-pool, patios and a gazebo with barbecue. Well-priced and well-furnished, these self-catering suites opened in 1995. In an up-market residential area near restaurants, shops.

❖ 148 Cleveland Drive, Lido Key, Sarasota, FL 34236 **Tel** (941) 383 9505; (800) 237 9505 **Fax** (941) 383 1830 **Meals** no meals served **Prices** rooms $$ **Rooms** 7, all with bath or shower, air-conditioning, phone, TV, VCR, kitchen **Credit cards** not accepted **Children** very welcome **Closed** never **Languages** English only

Cottage complex, Sarasota at Siesta Key

Turtle Beach Resort

Minutes from white, sandy beaches, these villas on the Intracoastal Waterway have simple, small rooms. Rather over-priced despite the swimming-pool, paddle boat and bicycles. Self-catering only, but there are three restaurants just next door.

❖ 9049 Midnight Pass Road, Siesta Key, FL 34242 **Tel** (941) 349 4554 **Fax** (941) 918 0203 **Meals** none served **Prices** rooms $$-$$$ **Rooms** 5, all with bath or shower, air-conditioning, phone, TV **Credit cards** AE, MC, V **Children** very welcome **Closed** never **Languages** English only

Central West

Restaurant with rooms, Sarasota at Siesta Key

The Wildflower Inn

Siesta Key is a quiet, mainly residential island. A few minutes from the beach, in a small shopping area, the Wildflower Café serves tasty vegetarian food. Upstairs are four light, airy, pretty bedrooms. This is a friendly place in an affluent community.

❖ 5218 Ocean Boulevard, Siesta Key, Sarasota, FL 34242 **Tel** (941) 346 1566 **Meals** breakfast, lunch, dinner **Prices** rooms $$ breakfast **Rooms** 4, all with bath or shower, air-conditioning, phone, TV, kitchen **Credit cards** MC, V **Children** welcome **Closed** never **Languages** English only

Artists' retreat, Tampa

Gram's Place

This eccentric music pub with rooms is named after the late country singer, Gram Parsons, who was a friend of the Rolling Stones. The bohemian style attracts gay and straight couples. There is a spa pool in the courtyard. Not a place for everyone.

❖ 3109 North Ola Ave, FL 33603 **Tel and Fax** (813) 221 0596 **Meals** breakfast, snacks **Prices** rooms $-$$ with breakfast **Rooms** 6, all with bath or shower, air-conditioning, phone, TV **Credit cards** AE,MC, V **Children** welcome **Closed** never **Languages** English only

Historic bed-and-breakfast, Tarpon Springs

Inness Manor

Named for the American father-and-son painters who once lived here and whose works are shown nearby, the house was restored in 1992 by Phyllis and George Rouhselang. Stunning woodwork, old-fashioned furniture and a homey atmosphere. Full breakfast.

❖ 34 West Orange Street, Tarpon Springs, FL 34689 **Tel** (813) 938 2900 **Meals** breakfast **Prices** rooms $-$$ with breakfast **Rooms** 6, 4 with bath or shower; all with air-conditioning **Credit cards** not accepted **Children** over 12 **Closed** never **Languages** English only

Historic house, Tarpon Springs

Spring Bayou Inn

Tarpon Springs has long had a lively Greek community based on sponge fishing. Grand vacation homes such as this, however, were built by wealthy northerners 100 years ago. In 1995, Sharon Birk took over the inn, with its grand fireplace and high ceilings.

❖ 32 West Tarpon Avenue, Tarpon Springs, FL 34689 **Tel** (813) 938 9333 **Meals** breakfast **Prices** rooms $-$$ with breakfast **Rooms** 5, 2 share bath or shower; all with air-conditioning **Credit cards** not accepted **Children** over12 **Closed** never **Languages** English only

Central

Horse Ranch, Altoona

Fiddler's Green Ranch

Essentially a dude ranch for horse lovers who want to ride in Ocala National Forest or even learn to ride. Self-catering only, in comfortable villas where short stays are possible. Child-friendly, home-on-the-range-style, with swimming-pool and tennis court.

❖ PO Box 70, Demko Road, Altoona, FL 32702 **Tel** (352) 669 7111; (800) 94 RANCH **Meals** not available **Prices** rooms $-$$$$ **Rooms** 4 villas, all with bath or shower, air-conditioning, TV, kitchen **Credit cards** MC, V **Children** very welcome **Closed** never **Languages** English only

Rural bed-and-breakfast, Astor

Little Creek Ranch

The ranch is still worked by Patsy Tatum's children while she concentrates on her 'Country Bed-and-Breakfast'. In Ocala National Forest, the informality appeals to those looking for peace but also to fans of auto racing at Daytona Speedway.

❖ PO Box 162, Astor, FL 32102 **Tel** (352) 759 2239 **Meals** breakfast **Prices** rooms $ with breakfast **Rooms** 3, all with bath or shower **Credit cards** not accepted **Children** welcome **Closed** never **Languages** English only

Rural ranch, Bushnell

Happy Wrangler Dude Ranch

In the middle of nowhere, horse lovers come to Carol and Rick Demme's ranch to ride in the huge state forest and canoe on a river. The log bunkhouse has simple, basic rooms and separate men's and women's bathrooms. Family-style dinners are served.

❖ Rt 2, PO Box 151A, Bushnell, FL 33513 **Tel** (352) 793 3833 **Meals** breakfast, lunch, dinner **Prices** rooms $ with breakfast **Rooms** 8, all share bath or shower; all with air-conditioning **Credit cards** MC, V **Children** very welcome **Closed** never **Languages** English only

Town bed-and-breakfast, Bushnell

Veranda House

Barbara Pownall came from Germany 35 years ago and now speaks English with an intriguing half-German, half-Southern accent. Her well-kept, 1888-house is in an out-of-the-way town, where guests fish and canoe nearby. A useful stop when touring.

❖ 202 West Noble Avenue, Bushnell, FL 33513 **Tel** (352) 793 3579 **Meals** breakfast **Prices** rooms $ with breakfast **Rooms** 2, both share bath or shower; both with air-conditioning **Credit cards** not accepted **Children** not suitable **Closed** never **Languages** German

Central

Restaurant with rooms, Haines City

Holly Garden Inn

Haines City is really just a village, half an hour away from Orlando's attractions. Opened in 1994 by young innkeepers Camilla and Wes Donnelly, bedrooms are stylish, comfortable. Full breakfast daily; their restaurant serves lunch on weekdays.

❖ 106 First Avenue South, Haines City, FL 33844 **Tel** (941) 421 9867 **Meals** breakfast, lunch **Prices** rooms $$ with breakfast **Rooms** 5, all with bath or shower, air-conditioning, phone, TV **Credit cards** AE, MC, V **Children** welcome **Closed** never **Languages** English only

Bed-and-breakfast, Kissimmee

The Unicorn Inn

An English couple, Fran and Don Williamson, opened up a 'typical British bed-and-breakfast' in 1993, after vacationing here. Their mixture of British prints and pottery fits well into the Colonial-style inn that makes a useful touring base for Orlando.

❖ 8 South Orlando Avenue, Kissimmee, FL 34741 **Tel** (407) 846 1200 **Fax** (407) 846 1773 **Meals** breakfast **Prices** rooms $ with breakfast **Rooms** 8, all with bath or shower, air-conditioning, TV, radio, hairdrier **Credit cards** MC, V **Children** welcome **Closed** never **Languages** English only

Town bed-and-breakfast, Lake Wales

Forget-Me-Not Bed & Breakfast

Lake Wales is the winter home of the Black Hills Passion Play, but the Bok Tower Gardens are a year-round attraction. Rebecca Hunter's veranda-wrapped 1914 house has five bedrooms named after flowers; they share three bathrooms. Afternoon tea served.

❖ 301 East Sessoms Avenue, Lake Wales, FL 33853 **Tel** (941) 676 5499 **Meals** breakfast, afternoon tea **Prices** rooms $$-$$$ with breakfast **Rooms** 5, sharing 3 bathrooms; all with air-conditioning, TV **Credit cards** MC, V **Children** welcome **Closed** never **Languages** English only

Spanish-style home, Lake Wales

Noah's Ark

Named after the owner, Noah Holton, whose pride and joy is his collection of European and American love seats. In a residential area, this large hacienda-style home, one of the oldest in Lake Wales, was a speakeasy during Prohibition. Open since 1993.

❖ 312 Ridge Manor Drive, Lake Wales, FL 33853 **Tel and Fax** (941) 676 1613; (800) 346 1613 **Meals** breakfast **Prices** rooms $$ with breakfast **Rooms** 7, all with bath or shower, air-conditioning **Credit cards** MC, V **Children** welcome **Closed** never **Languages** English only

Central

Restaurant with rooms, Lakeland

Magnolias Inn the Park

Restaurateur Tim Alward worked all over the USA, but in 1995 returned to his roots in this small, pleasant town known for its antiques shops. In the heart of downtown, the four-poster beds in pretty rooms suit business travellers as well as shoppers.

❖ 255 North Kentucky Avenue, Lakeland, FL 33801 **Tel** (941) 686 7275 **Fax** (941) 683 6443 **Meals** breakfast, lunch, snacks **Prices** rooms $$ with breakfast **Rooms** 4, all with bath or shower, air-conditioning, phone, radio **Credit cards** MC, V **Children** welcome **Closed** never **Languages** English only

Lakeside bed-and-breakfast, Minneola

Lake Minneola Inn

On one of 13 lakes linked by canals, guests rent boats, fish, sail and swim. Bill Parrish's turn-of-the-century building needs painting outside but the interior is well-kept and some bedrooms have handsome antiques. A 30-min drive from Orlando.

❖ 508 Maine Avenue, PO Box 803, Minneola, FL 34755 **Tel** (352) 394 2232 **Meals** breakfast **Prices** rooms $ with breakfast **Rooms** 9, all with bath or shower, air-conditioning, phone, TV **Credit cards** MC, V **Children** over 5 **Closed** never **Languages** English only

Bed-and-breakfast, Mount Dora

Christopher's Inn

A visit to Jack and Inez Simpson is like a trip back to the 1920s. They serve an old-fashioned sit-down breakfast in the dining-room of their family home, on the edge of downtown by Gilbert Park. Renovated in 1994, all bedrooms have separate entrances.

❖ 539 Liberty Avenue, Mount Dora, FL 32757 **Tel** (352) 383 2244 **Meals** breakfast **Prices** rooms $$ with breakfast **Rooms** 4, all with bath or shower, air-conditioning **Credit cards** AE, MC, V **Children** over 12 **Closed** never **Languages** English only

Country bed-and-breakfast, Mount Dora

Emerald Hill Inn

When Mount Dora is crowded with antiques hunters, this inn, deep in the orange groves and overlooking Lake Victoria, is a welcome retreat. The Wisemans' decorator background shows in the fancy bedrooms. Health-conscious breakfasts.

❖ 27751 Lake Jem Road, Mount Dora, FL 32757 **Tel** (352) 383 2777 **Meals** breakfast **Prices** rooms $$-$$$ with breakfast **Rooms** 4, 2 share bath or shower; all have air-conditioning **Credit cards** MC, V **Children** over 10 **Closed** never **Languages** English only

Central

Bed-and-breakfast, Mount Dora

Farnsworth House

The century-old house with its shade trees and garden could do with a facelift. Regulars, however, remain loyal, mainly due to Dick Shelton's friendly and attentive manner which goes a long way to overshadow the house's shortcomings. Quiet setting.

❖ 1029 East 5th Ave, Mount Dora, FL 32757 **Tel** (352) 735 1894 **Meals** breakfast **Prices** rooms $$ with breakfast **Rooms** 5, all with bath or shower, air-conditioning **Credit cards** MC, V **Children** welcome **Closed** never **Languages** English only

Bed-and-breakfast, Mount Dora

Raintree House

Dottie Smith's modern, sprawling Florida bungalow has views of Lake Dora. Crisp and clean interior with a few antiques but no lacy trappings. Cool and breezy back yard, with the usual screened back porch. Within walking distance of antique shops.

❖ 1123 Dora Way, Mount Dora, FL 32757 **Tel** (352) 383 5065 **Fax** (352) 383 1920 **Meals** breakfast **Prices** rooms $$ with breakfast **Rooms** 3, 2 share bath or shower; all with air-conditioning **Credit cards** MC, V **Children** over 13 **Closed** never **Languages** English only

Historic house, Mount Dora

Seabrook Bed & Breakfast

Although right in the heart of the downtown area of Mount Dora with its antiques and crowds, the 100-year old house is a rather expensive place to stay. Bedrooms are crammed with objects and colours to create atmosphere. Wheelchair access.

❖ 644 North Donnelly Street, PO Box 1301, Mount Dora, FL 32757 **Tel** (352) 383 4800 **Meals** breakfast **Prices** rooms $$-$$$ with breakfast **Rooms** 6, all with bath or shower, air-conditioning, phone, TV **Credit cards** MC, V **Children** welcome **Closed** never **Languages** English only

Bed-and-breakfast, Mount Dora

Simpson's Bed & Breakfast

The prize for being closest to the shops goes to Simpson's, with four rooms above a florist. Expect no extras; breakfast arrives in a basket in your room, furnishings are a mix that rarely match. A useful overnight stay if all the other places in town are full up.

❖ 441 North Donnelly Street, Mount Dora, FL 32757 **Tel** (352) 383 2087 **Meals** breakfast **Prices** rooms $$ with breakfast **Suites** 2, both with bath or shower, air-conditioning, phone, TV, kitchen **Credit cards** MC, V **Children** welcome **Closed** never **Languages** English only

Central

Rural ranch, Ocklawaha

Wit's End Farm

Owner Margo Atwood Langstaff, who once rode a horse across the USA, now raises horses by Lake Fay. A two-bedroom suite suits guests looking for seclusion. They take carriage rides, swim, fish, and canoe in the lake, or hike in Ocala National Forest.

❖ PO Box 964, Ocklawaha, FL 32179 **Tel** (352) 288 4924 **Fax** (352) 288 2800 **Meals** breakfast **Prices** rooms $-$$ with breakfast **Rooms** 1, with bath, air-conditioning, kitchen **Credit Cards** not accepted **Children** very welcome **Closed** never **Languages** English only

Country inn, St Cloud

Hunter Arms

This 60-year old hotel is 20 minutes from Orlando's airport, yet just a short walk from Lake Toho, in the old part of St Cloud. Ann Williams offers remarkable value: attentive service, recently-refurbished rooms, and competent food in the restaurant.

❖ 1029 New York Avenue, St Cloud, FL 34769 **Tel** (407) 891 1688 **Fax** (407) 891 1987 **Meals** breakfast, lunch **Prices** rooms $ with breakfast **Rooms** 34, all with bath or shower, air-conditioning, phone, TV **Credit cards** MC, V **Children** very welcome **Closed** never **Languages** English only

Bed-and-breakfast, Sanford

The Higgins House

Sanford is a handy base for Orlando or Daytona Beach, and a pleasant town. Roberta and Walter Padgett's 100-year old blue clapboard house follows a Victorian theme, with stencilling on floors and ceilings. A separate cottage offers privacy for a family.

❖ 420 South Oak Ave, Sanford, FL 32771 **Tel** (407) 324 9238; (800) 584 0014 **Meals** breakfast **Prices** rooms $-$$ with breakfast **Rooms** 4, all with bath or shower, air-conditioning, phone, TV **Credit cards** AE, MC, V **Children** over 12 **Closed** never **Languages** English only

Ranch house, Sebring

Double M Ranch

The Matheny family business gives a glimpse of Florida before tourism became an industry. Timber, cattle and citrus orchards surround the ranch. One room is themed with artwork from London, the other from Malaysia. Come to canoe, ride, or fish.

❖ Rte 1, Box 292, Zolfo Springs, Sebring, FL 33890 **Tel** (941) 735 0266 **Meals** breakfast **Prices** rooms $ with breakfast **Rooms** 2, both with bath or shower, air-conditioning **Credit cards** not accepted **Children** not suitable **Closed** never **Languages** English only

Central

Town hotel, Sebring

Santa Rosa Inn & Café

Jan and Don Bowden run this plush combination of hotel and restaurant in the heart of Sebring's old downtown area. Antique and reproduction furniture give the old-fashioned feel, both in bedrooms and the Café. The beds are particularly comfortable.

❖ 509 North Ridgewood Drive, Sebring, FL 33870 **Tel** (941) 385 0641
Meals breakfast, lunch, dinner **Prices** rooms $-$$ with breakfast
Rooms 25, all with bath or shower, air-conditioning, phone, TV
Credit cards AE, MC, V **Children** welcome **Closed** never
Languages English only

Bed-and-breakfast, Tavares

Fleur du Lac

Just west of Mt Dora, overlooking Lake Dora, this is an elegant Colonial-style home, filled with antiques. Wood floors, leaded window panes. The Eastwoods grow their own organic produce for breakfasts. Swimming-pool, garden with huge oaks.

❖ 426 Lake Dora Drive, Tavares, FL 32778 **Tel** (352) 343 0046
Meals breakfast **Prices** rooms $$ with breakfast **Rooms** 4, 3 share bath or shower; all with air-conditioning **Credit cards** not accepted
Children welcome **Closed** never **Languages** English only

Central East

Luxury inn, Daytona Beach

Coquina Inn

Joe Witek and Craig Heidel took over this well-known bed-and-breakfast in 1995 and plan to enlarge it to seven rooms. Built of coquina rock in 1912, the well-restored building has glamourous antiques, including a piano. Quiet, but no swimming-pool.

❖ 544 South Palmetto Avenue, Daytona Beach, FL 32114 **Tel** (904) 254 4969; (800) 805 7533 **Meals** breakfast **Prices** rooms $$ with breakfast **Rooms** 4, all with bath or shower, air-conditioning, phone, TV **Credit cards** AE, MC, V **Children** not suitable **Closed** never **Languages** English only

Ocean-side hotel, Daytona Beach Shores

Captain's Quarters

A small family-owned high-rise right on Daytona's excellent beach. Rooms are plain, generic and simple. The Galley serves breakfast, lunch. Friends sharing a suite find this particularly well-priced. Popular for Speedway race weeks. Swimming-pool.

❖ 3711 South Atlantic Avenue, Daytona Beach Shores, FL 32127 **Tel** (904) 767 3119; (800) 332 3119 **Fax** (904) 767 0883 **Meals** breakfast, lunch, snacks **Prices** rooms $$-$$$ **Suites** 26, all with bath or shower, air-conditioning, phone, TV **Credit cards** AE, MC, V **Children** welcome **Closed** never **Languages** English only

Rural bed-and-breakfast, DeLand

DeLand Country Inn

Disarmingly simple, this turn-of-the-century house with a big porch is a viable alternative to the motels that abound. With plenty of land and a swimming-pool, this appeals to families with children who need space to play. Relaxed and well-priced.

❖ 228 West Howry Avenue, DeLand, FL 32720 **Tel** (904) 736 4244 **Meals** breakfast **Prices** rooms $-$$ with breakfast **Rooms** 5, all with bath or shower, air-conditioning **Credit cards** AE, MC, V **Children** welcome **Closed** never **Languages** English only

Other recommendations

❖ **Edgewater**: Colonial House Bed and Breakfast, 110 East Yelkca Terrace, Edgewater, FL 32132. Tel and Fax (904) 427 4570. $-$$. 4 rooms. German-owned, with swimming-pool and Jacuzzi. Between Cape Canaveral and Daytona Beach.

❖ **New Smyrna Beach**: Indian River Inn, 1210 South Riverside Drive, New Smyrna Beach, FL 32168. Tel (904) 428 2491; (800) 541 4529. Fax (904) 426 2532. $-$$. 42 rooms. Bustling, business-like, on the Indian River, with swimming-pool, fishing.

Northwest

Apartments, Cedar Key

The Island Place

Linked by causeway to the mainland, this island remains low-key and undeveloped, with few beaches but nature reserves nearby. These four low attractive buildings stand right on the water, near restaurants and main boat dock. Notable comfort, well-priced.

❖ PO Box 687, Cedar Key, FL 32625 **Tel** (352) 543 5307; (800) 780 6522 **Fax** (352) 543 9141 **Meals** not served **Prices** rooms $$ **Rooms** 28, all with bath or shower, air-conditioning, phone, TV, kitchen **Credit cards** AE, MC, V **Children** very welcome **Closed** never **Languages** English only

Beach motel, Destin

Frangista Beach Inn

Since the 1995 hurricane, a new road bypasses this ever-expanding motel, set on a bluff above the Gulf shore. Completely refurbished, with the new Seafood and Spirits restaurant across the street. Quiet, useful for family beach vacations.

❖ 1860 Old Highway 98, Destin, FL 32541 **Tel** (904) 654 5501; (800) 382 2612 **Fax** (904) 654 5876 **Meals** breakfast, lunch, dinner **Prices** rooms $$-$$$ with breakfast **Rooms** 57, all with bath or shower, air-conditioning, kitchenettes, phone, TV **Credit cards** AE, MC, V **Children** very welcome **Closed** never **Languages** English only

Bed-and-breakfast, Havana

Gaver's Bed & Breakfast

Shirley and Bruce Gaver have a cheery, recently-redecorated, 1907 cottage, furnished with souvenirs of their travels: toys, antiques and art. The Cherry Room has a fine pencil-post bed. A pleasant overnight stay in a town best known for its antiques.

❖ 301 East 6th Avenue, Havana, FL 32333 **Tel and Fax** (904) 539 5611 **Meals** breakfast **Prices** rooms $$ with breakfast **Rooms** 2, both with bath or shower, air-conditioning **Credit cards** not accepted **Children** over 8 **Closed** never **Languages** English only

Gulfside inn, Mexico Beach

Driftwood Inn

Wedged between the highway and the Gulf shore, the modern Victorian-style houses and beach cottages are ideal for families, with contemporary furniture and beds beneath the bright red corrugated tin roofs. Peggy Wood is an outgoing hostess.

❖ 2105 Highway 98, On The Beach, PO Box 13447, Mexico Beach, FL 32410 **Tel** (904) 648 5126 **Fax** (904) 648 8505 **Meals** breakfast **Prices** rooms $-$$$ with breakfast **Rooms** 20, all with bath or shower, air-conditioning, phone, TV, kitchen **Credit cards** MC, V **Children** very welcome **Closed** never **Languages** English only

Northwest

Historic house, Monticello

Palmer Place

Popular for its antique shops and historic district, Monticello is worth a visit. Set in vast gardens, the Hawkins' home is also spacious within, with a grand piano, massive canopied beds and chunky antique furniture to give a real flavour of Southern life.

❖ 625 West Palmer Mill Road, Monticello, FL 32345 **Tel** (904) 997 5519 **Meals** breakfast **Prices** rooms $-$$ with breakfast **Rooms** 5, all with bath or shower, air-conditioning **Credit cards** AE, MC, V **Children** welcome **Closed** never **Languages** English only

Beach house, St Teresa Beach

Sand Dollar Bed & Breakfast

Staying with Muriel Crusoe is like staying at Granny's beach house with its huge shell collection. Small bedrooms, but a vast unspoiled beach at the door. Breakfasts for heroes include fruit, eggs, meats, Southern-style grits and scratch biscuits. Fun.

❖ Rte 1, Box 460, St Teresa Beach, Sopchoppy, FL 32358 **Tel** (904) 697 2652 **Meals** breakfast **Prices** rooms $$ with breakfast **Rooms** 2, both with bath or shower, air-conditioning, TV **Credit cards** not accepted **Children** not suitable **Closed** Christmas and New Year **Languages** English only

Gulfside inn, Seagrove Beach

Sugar Beach Inn

Just across the street from the fine white sand beach that gives the house its name, the inn is within walking distance of Seaside, the mock Victorian village. Large verandas outside, American and British antiques within add up to sophistication by the sea.

❖ 3501 East Scenic 30-A, Seagrove Beach, FL 32459 **Tel and Fax** (904) 231 1577 **Meals** breakfast **Prices** rooms $$-$$$ with breakfast **Rooms** 3, all with bath or shower, air-conditioning, phone, TV **Credit cards** MC, V **Children** not suitable **Closed** never **Languages** English only

Bed-and-breakfast, Tallahassee

The Riedel House

Carolyn Riedel has built up a fine reputation for her home in the state capital. Although a change of ownership is possible, we hope that the 60-year old house with its terraced gardens near the country club will remain as elegant as ever.

❖ 1412 Fairway Drive, Tallahasse, FL 32301 **Tel** (904) 222 8569 **Meals** breakfast **Prices** rooms $$ with breakfast **Rooms** 3, all with bath or shower, air-conditioning **Credit cards** not accepted **Children** not suitable **Closed** never **Languages** English only

Northwest

Thomasville, Georgia

Less than an hour's drive north of Tallahassee, just over the Georgia border, is Thomasville, known as the City of Roses. Well worth a visit by anyone touring the north-west of Florida, the grandeur of the late 19thC winter resort remains, along with about 50 'winter cottages' for the rich Northerners who used to travel south to thaw out. Just to the south is Pebble Hill Plantation, a fine example of the private estates that survived the Civil War. Many of the inns and bed-and-breakfasts offer Southern food, furnishing and hospitality. Best of all, there are no parking meters on the brick streets of a town that also boasts some quality antiques shops.

Bed-and-breakfast, Thomasville

1884 Paxton House

Susie Sherrod is determinedly romantic. Her Victorian Gothic inn has fireplaces and chandeliers plus her collections of teapots and dolls. The suites in the Garden Cottage offer seclusion. Right in the historic downtown, this is a strictly non-smoking inn.

❖ 445 Remington Avenue, Thomasville, GA 31792 **Tel** (912) 226 5197; (800) 278 0138 **Meals** breakfast **Prices** rooms $-$$$ with breakfast **Rooms** 6, all with bath or shower, air-conditioning, phone, TV, radio; some VCR **Credit cards** AE, MC, V **Children** over 12 **Closed** never **Languages** English only

Victorian home, Thomasville

Evans House Bed and Breakfast

John and Lee Puskar's grand century-old home facing Paradise Park is furnished in Victorian style. The parlor and dining-room, where a full breakfast is served, are formal. Professionally-run; suitable for business travellers. Walking distance to the shops.

❖ 725 South Hansell Street, Thomasville, GA 31792 **Tel** (912) 226 1343; (800) 344 4717 **Fax** (912) 226 0653 **Meals** breakfast **Prices** rooms $-$$ with breakfast **Rooms** 4, all with bath or shower, air-conditioning **Credit cards** not accepted **Children** not suitable **Closed** never **Languages** English only

Bed-and-breakfast, Thomasville

The Grand Victoria Inn

Anne Dodge is the lively innkeeper in this attractive home just south of the Victorian downtown area. With its white picket fence and deep porch, the Grand Victoria has contemporary as well as antique touches. Light, large bedrooms. Full breakfast.

❖ 817 South Hansell Street, Thomasville, GA 31792 **Tel** (912) 226 7460 **Fax** (912) 228 8588 **Meals** breakfast **Prices** rooms $-$$ with breakfast **Rooms** 4, all with bath or shower, air-conditioning **Credit cards** not accepted **Children** welcome **Closed** never **Languages** English only

Northwest

Bed-and-breakfast, Thomasville

Our Cottage on the Park

In her yellow pine, Victorian house overlooking Paradise Park, Constance Clineman likes to cook elaborate breakfast dishes such as Quiche à la Edward, served on Royal Doulton china. Relaxed, with freshly-baked brownies to seduce visitors at tea.

❖ 801 South Hansell Street, Thomasville, GA 31792 **Tel** (912) 227 0404
Meals breakfast, snacks **Prices** rooms $ with breakfast
Rooms 2, all with bath or shower **Credit cards** not accepted
Children welcome **Closed** never **Languages** English only

Town bed-and-breakfast, Thomasville

Serendipity Cottage

Beautifully built of oak, thanks to the first owner who was a lumber merchant, Kathy and Ed Middleton's handsome 1906 home is in the Dawson Street Historic District, near several antiques shops. Breakfasts are a major feature. Well-priced.

❖ 339 East Jefferson Street, Thomasville, GA 31792 **Tel** (912) 226 8111
Meals breakfast **Prices** rooms $-$$ with breakfast
Rooms 3, 2 with bath or shower, air-conditioning, phone, TV
Credit cards not accepted **Children** not suitable **Closed** never
Languages English only

Ante-bellum mansion, Thomasville

Susina Plantation Inn

Anne-Marie Walker's splendid 1841 Greek Revival mansion is almost on the Florida border. A vast estate, complete with swimming-pool, tennis courts, fishing. Bedrooms have fine antiques; a five-course dinner is included in price of a night's stay.

❖ Rte 3, Box 1010, 1420 Meridian Road, Thomasville, GA 31792
Tel (912) 377 9644 **Meals** breakfast, dinner **Prices** rooms $$$-$$$$
with breakfast,dinner **Rooms** 8, all with bath or shower, air-conditioning
Credit cards not accepted **Children** welcome **Closed** never
Languages English only

Other recommendations

❖ **Thomasville**: Deer Creek B&B, 1304 Old Monticello Road, Thomasville, GA 31792. Tel (912) 226 7294. $. 1 large room. Modern, with picture windows. Next to golf course. Some antiques.

❖ **Thomasville**: Moss Oaks B&B, PO Box 2011, Thomasville, GA 31799. Tel (912) 377 6280; (800) 377 1102. $. 2 rooms. 1903 house deep in the country, west of town.

❖ **Thomasville**: South Woods Bobwhite B&B, Rte 1, Box 429A, Thomasville, GA 31792. Tel: (912) 226 0170. $. 4 rooms. Outside town, in country. Dinner by request.

Northeast

Bed-and-breakfast, Amelia Island

The 1735 House

Although Emily and Gary Grables' inn is a long-established family favourite for seaside holidays, the weathered house needs a thorough facelift to compete with livelier local rivals. Breakfast is served in bedrooms in a basket. Seabreeze is the best room.

❖ 584 South Fletcher Avenue, Amelia Island, FL 32034
Tel (904) 261 5878; (800) 872 8531 **Meals** breakfast **Prices** rooms $$-$$$ with breakfast **Rooms** 5, all with bath or shower, air-conditioning **Credit cards** AE, MC, V **Children** welcome **Closed** never **Languages** English only

Historic hotel, Amelia Island

Florida House Inn

Although proud owners of Florida's oldest surviving hotel (1857), the Warners have let standards slip. Plastic carpet on the front steps, plastic covers on dining-tables, impersonal bedrooms. Prettier and better-priced rivals are on the island.

❖ 20 & 22 South 3rd Street, PO Box 688, Amelia Island, FL 32034
Tel (904) 261 3300; (800) 258 3301 **Meals** breakfast, lunch, dinner **Prices** rooms $-$$$ with breakfast **Rooms** 11, all with bath or shower, air-conditioning, phone, TV **Credit cards** AE, MC, V **Children** welcome **Closed** never **Languages** English only

Cottage suites, Amelia Island

The Taber House

Frances and Bo Taber have travelled the world, so their two cottages, one modern, the other 150 years old, are filled with memorabilia. The interiors do have charm, but squeezed between offices and a parking lot, this is an expensive experience.

❖ 15 North 4th Street, PO Box 734, Fernandina Beach, Amelia Island, FL 32035 **Tel** (904) 261 6391 **Meals** breakfast **Prices** rooms $$-$$$ with breakfast **Suites** 3, all with bath or shower, air-conditioning, phone, TV **Credit cards** not accepted **Children** not suitable **Closed** never **Languages** English only

Ranch, Branford

Quina's Funny Farm

An eccentric name for the 80-acre (35 ha) farm where Kitty and Steve Quina raise deer. Simple, homey house. Guests hike in woods, ride bicycles, go antique hunting in High Springs 8 miles 14 km) to the east. Water sports in nearby state parks.

❖ Route 2, Box 389, Branford, FL 32008 **Tel** (904) 935 3320
Fax (904) 935 2941 **Meals** breakfast **Prices** rooms $-$$ with breakfast **Rooms** 2, both with bath or shower, air-conditioning **Credit cards** MC, V **Children** over 12 **Closed** never **Languages** English only

Northeast

Riverside house, High Springs

Ichetucknee River Tree House

You're on your own in a remote, magical setting. This three-bedroom tree house stands on stilts among woods filled with wildlife. A walkway leads down to the river, used for canoeing, fishing. Well-equipped for self-catering, so who needs a host?

❖ c/o The Great Outdoors Trading Company, 65 North Main Street, PO Box 387, High Springs, FL 32643 **Tel** (904) 454 2900 **Fax** (904) 454 7389 **Meals** no meals served **Price** $$$ **House** with bath or shower, air-conditioning, phone, TV **Credit cards** MC, V **Children** very welcome **Closed** never **Languages** English only

Town bed-and-breakfast, High Springs

The Spring House

This handsome house has the Southern trappings of live oaks in the yard, a deep porch and swing seats. Inside are fine Victorian architectural features: towering ceilings, fine wood floors. The Gabriels, a young couple with a baby, also organise bike tours.

❖ 211 South Main Street, PO Box 2257, High Springs, FL 32643 **Tel** (904) 454 8571 **Meals** breakfast **Prices** rooms $-$$ with breakfast **Rooms** 3, all with bath or shower, air-conditioning **Credit cards** MC, V **Children** over 8 **Closed** never **Languages** English only

Town bed-and-breakfast, Lake Butler

Old Townsend House

Business visitors and locals who want a Victorian experience book into this restored 19thC house with its original mouldings, 14 doors, and porches front and back. Clint and Sally Clausel offer Southern hospitality 30 miles (48 km) north of Gainesville.

❖ 235 SW Fourth Avenue, Lake Butler, FL 32054 **Tel** (904) 496 1187 **Meals** breakfast **Prices** rooms $ with breakfast **Rooms** 4, all with bath or shower, air-conditioning **Credit cards** AE, MC, V **Children** over 12 **Closed** never **Languages** English only

Bed-and-breakfast, St Augustine

Agustín Inn

Despite the busy pedestrian traffic, the inn remains peaceful behind a high fence. Although Vanessa Cushman has only been here since 1994, her breakfasts are praised. Room 1 is handicap-equipped; room 6 has a pretty balcony over the front yard.

❖ 29 Cuna Street, St Augustine, FL 32084 **Tel** (904) 823 9559; (800) 248 7846 **Meals** breakfast **Prices** rooms $$ with breakfast **Rooms** 7, all with bath or shower, air-conditioning **Credit cards** AE, MC, V **Children** not suitable **Closed** never **Languages** English only

Northeast

Bed-and-breakfast, St Augustine

Alexander Homestead

Since 1992, Bonnie Alexander has focused on romance in her cottage, where guests can order champagne, antique glasses, fruit and cheese for a getaway weekend. Nearer Flagler College than Historic District. A standby, if in need of pampering.

❖ 14 Seville Street, St Augustine, FL 32084 **Tel** (904) 826 4147; (800) 555 4147 **Fax** (904) 823 9503 **Meals** breakfast **Prices** rooms $$-$$$ with breakfast **Rooms** 4, all with bath or shower, air-conditioning **Credit cards** AE, MC, V **Children** welcome **Closed** never **Languages** English only

Bed-and-breakfast, St Augustine

Castle Garden

This was once the carriage-house of the mansion across the street that is now the popular museum called Ripley's Believe It or Not. Since Bruce Kloeckner made the conversion in 1991, he has added two luxury suites with Jacuzzis. Near the old fort.

❖ 15 Shenandoah Street, St Augustine, FL 32084 **Tel** (904) 829 3839 **Meals** breakfast **Prices** rooms $$ with breakfast **Rooms** 6, all with bath or shower, air-conditioning **Credit cards** MC, V **Children** over 6 **Closed** never **Languages** English only

Bed-and-breakfast, St Augustine

Cordova House

Carole and Hal Schroeder's Colonial Revival home is a simple, unpretentious spot to stay. The main draw here is the swimming-pool plus a hot tub in the gazebo. Richard's Room is the prettiest, with well-matched paper and fabrics. Own car parking.

❖ 16 Cordova Street, St Augustine, FL 32084 **Tel** (904) 825 0770 **Fax** (904) 823 1330 **Meals** breakfast **Prices** rooms $$ with breakfast **Rooms** 3, all with bath or shower, air-conditioning, TV **Credit cards** MC, V **Children** over 10 **Closed** never **Languages** English only

Bed-and-breakfast, St Augustine

Our House of St Augustine

John and Virginia Erfmann's small house is on a quiet street in the Antique District, just outside the Historic District. First impressions include a tidy clipped lawn behind a picket fence. Bedrooms are equally neat, with just a few floral splashes.

❖ 7 Cincinnati Avenue, St Augustine, FL 32084 **Tel** (904) 824 9204 **Meals** breakfast **Prices** rooms $$ with breakfast **Rooms** 3, all with bath or shower, air-conditioning **Credit cards** not accepted **Children** not suitable **Closed** never **Languages** English only

Northeast

Historic inn, St Augustine

St Francis Inn

Despite its 200-year history, there is no excuse for the recent and marked drop in standards: worn decoration, unmatched furniture, old-fashioned plumbing. Despite manager Beverly Lonergan's cheerfulness, better value can be had nearby.

❖ 279 St George Street, St Augustine, FL 32084 **Tel** (904) 824 6068; (800) 824 6062 **Meals** breakfast **Prices** rooms $-$$$ with breakfast **Rooms** 12, all with bath or shower, air-conditioning, TV **Credit cards** MC, V **Children** very welcome **Closed** never **Languages** English only

Bed-and-breakfast, St Augustine

Segui Inn

George Lent claims he sticks to "cooking and janitoring", while his wife, Nikki, looks after guests. Their home celebrates her family, with great-grandparents' dining-room furniture and rooms named after her mother and daughter. On a busy road.

❖ 47 San Marco Avenue, St Augustine, FL 32084 **Tel** (904) 825 2811 **Fax** (904) 824 3967 **Meals** breakfast **Prices** rooms $$-$$$ with breakfast **Rooms** 4, all with bath or shower, air-conditioning **Credit cards** MC, V **Children** welcome **Closed** never **Languages** English only

Bed-and-breakfast, St Augustine

Whale's Tale

Denis and Betty Cunningham have followed a Moby Dick theme for the rooms in their inn: 'Melville' has views of the bay; 'Ishmail' is quiet, in pinks and blues. Not too frilly, but convenient, clean and fair value for money. Well-run, with hearty breakfasts.

❖ 54 Charlotte Street, St Augustine, FL 32084 **Tel** (904) 829 5901 **Meals** breakfast **Prices** rooms $-$$ with breakfast **Rooms** 7, all with bath or shower, air-conditioning **Credit cards** MC, V **Children** welcome **Closed** never **Languages** English only

Bed-and-breakfast, San Mateo

Ferncourt

Time has passed San Mateo by, and Jack Morgan's 100-year old home remains Victorian, with its wrap-around porch and comfortable bedrooms. Breakfast is a strong point, thanks to home-made jams, breads and even rice pudding and soufflés.

❖ PO Box 758, San Mateo, FL 32187 **Tel** (904) 329 9755 **Meals** breakfast **Prices** rooms $ with breakfast **Rooms** 5, all with bath or shower, air-conditioning **Credit cards** AE, MC, V **Children** welcome **Closed** never **Languages** English only

Index of hotel names

Index of hotel names

Index of hotel names

Index of hotel names

Index of hotel names

Index of hotel locations

Index of hotel locations

Index of hotel locations

Index of hotel locations

Special offers

Buy your ***Charming Small Hotel Guide*** by post directly from the publisher and you'll get a worthwhile discount. *

Titles available:	*Retail price*	*Discount price*
Austria	£7.99	**£6.00**
Britain & Ireland	£9.99	**£7.00**
USA: Florida	£9.99	**£7.00**
France	£9.99	**£7.00**
France: *Bed & Breakfast*	£8.99	**£6.50**
Germany	£8.99	**£6.50**
Italy	£8.99	**£6.50**
USA: New England	£8.99	**£6.50**
Spain	£8.99	**£6.50**
Switzerland	£7.99	**£6.00**
Tuscany & Umbria	£9.99	**£7.00**

If you like *Charming Small Hotel Guides* you'll also enjoy Duncan Petersen's ***Versatile Guides:*** outstanding all-purpose travel guides written by authors, not by committee.

Titles available:	*Retail price*	*Discount price*
California *The Versatile Guide*	£12.99	**£8.75**
Central Italy *The Versatile Guide*	£12.99	**£8.75**
France *The Versatile Guide*	£12.99	**£8.75**
Greece *The Versatile Guide*	£12.99	**£8.75**
Italy *The Versatile Guide*	£12.99	**£8.75**
Spain *The Versatile Guide*	£12.99	**£8.75**
Thailand *The Versatile Guide*	£12.99	**£8.75**
Turkey *The Versatile Guide*	£12.99	**£8.75**

Please send your order to:

***Book Sales*, Duncan Petersen Publishing Ltd,**

31 Ceylon Road, London W14 OYP

enclosing: 1) the title you require and number of copies

2) your name and address

3) your cheque made out to:

Duncan Petersen Publishing Ltd

**Offer applies to UK only.*

Special Offers

CHARMING SMALL HOTEL GUIDES

Would you like to receive information about special discounts at hotels in the ***Charming Small Hotel Guide*** series?

☆

Many of our hotels are offering big savings on standard room rates if you book at certain times of the year.

☆

If so, send your name and address to:

Reader Information
Charming Small Hotel Guides
Duncan Petersen Publishing
31 Ceylon Road
London W14 OYP

☆

For more offers see page 191